Gooseberry Patch

A Country Store In Your Mailbox®

Come on Over

A Country Store In Your Mailbox®

Gooseberry Patch
600 London Road
Department Book
Delaware, OH 43015

★

1·800·854·6673

www.gooseberrypatch.com

Copyright 2004, Gooseberry Patch 1-931890-41-2
Fifth Printing, January, 2006

Do you have a tried & true recipe...

tip, craft or memory that you'd like to see featured in a **Gooseberry Patch** book? Visit our website at **www.gooseberrypatch.com**, register and follow the easy steps to submit your favorite family recipe. Or send them to us at:

Gooseberry Patch
Attn: Book Dept.
P.O. Box 190
Delaware, OH 43015

Don't forget to include the number of servings your recipe makes, plus your name, street address, phone number and e-mail address. If we select your recipe, your name will appear right along with it...and you'll receive a **FREE** copy of the book!

Contents

Dedication

For everyone who enjoys cozy get-togethers around the table.

Appreciation

To our friends who shared their recipes that make everyone feel like family...thank you!

Breezy Breakfasts

Welcome!

Overnight Coffee Cake

Jennie Wiseman
Coshocton, OH

Company on their way? Bake right away, it's not necessary to chill.

1 c. all-purpose flour
1/4 c. sugar
1/4 c. brown sugar, packed
1/2 t. baking soda
1/2 t. baking powder

1/2 t. cinnamon
1/2 c. buttermilk
1/3 c. margarine
1 egg

Combine all ingredients; mix well. Spread in a greased 9" round cake pan; cover with plastic wrap and refrigerate overnight. Sprinkle with topping; bake at 350 degrees for 20 to 25 minutes. Drizzle with glaze. Serves 8.

Topping:

1/4 c. brown sugar, packed
1/4 c. chopped nuts

1/2 t. cinnamon
1/4 t. nutmeg

Toss all ingredients together.

Glaze:

1/2 c. powdered sugar
1/4 t. vanilla extract

3 to 4 t. milk

Combine powdered sugar and vanilla; stir in enough milk to reach desired consistency.

Breezy Breakfasts

Sunrise Cinnamon Loaves

Nichole Martelli
Alvin, TX

Make 'em mini loaves so every guest has their own. This recipe will make five, 6"x3" mini loaves...just shorten bake time to 35 minutes.

18-1/2 oz. pkg. yellow cake mix
   with pudding
4 eggs
3/4 c. oil

3/4 c. water
1 t. vanilla extract
1/2 c. sugar
3 T. cinnamon

Blend the first 5 ingredients together on high speed of an electric mixer for 3 minutes; divide batter in half. Equally divide one half and pour into 2 greased and floured 8"x4" loaf pans; set aside. Combine sugar and cinnamon in a small bowl; sprinkle half evenly over the batter in each loaf pan. Spread remaining batter evenly into each loaf pan; sprinkle loaves with remaining sugar and cinnamon. Use a knife to gently swirl sugar and cinnamon into batter; bake at 350 degrees for 45 minutes. Cool on wire racks. Makes 16 servings.

A glassful of fresh-squeezed orange juice is always
a treat at breakfast. Set out a juicer along with
a bowl of oranges cut in half so guests can take
a turn at squeezing their own.

Yummy Caramel French Toast

The Doubleday Inn
Gettysburg, PA

Slice bread into sticks before baking...the kids will love dipping them into syrup.

1 c. brown sugar, packed
1/2 c. margarine
2 T. corn syrup
8 slices Italian bread
6 eggs, lightly beaten

1-1/2 c. milk
1 t. vanilla extract
1/8 t. salt
Garnish: warm syrup

Combine the first 3 ingredients in a saucepan; bring to a full boil. Reduce heat; simmer until thickened, about 2 to 3 minutes. Pour in a greased 13"x9" baking pan; arrange bread slices in a single layer on top. Set aside. Combine eggs with remaining ingredients; mix well. Pour over bread slices; cover with aluminum foil and refrigerate overnight. Uncover and bake at 350 degrees until golden, about 45 minutes; drizzle with syrup before serving. Makes 8 servings.

Hosting a Mothers' Day Brunch or a Girls' Tea Party? Dress up the table by tying pretty scarves around chair backs, then tuck a tulip in each knot.

Breezy Breakfasts

German Apple Pancake

Marilyn Williams
Westerville, OH

Jonathan or McIntosh apples are the tastiest to use in this recipe.

1/4 c. butter
1-1/2 t. cinnamon, divided
2 apples, cored, peeled and
    thinly sliced
3 eggs, beaten
1/2 c. frozen apple juice
    concentrate, thawed

1/2 c. all-purpose flour
1/4 c. half-and-half
1-1/2 t. vanilla extract
1/4 t. nutmeg
1/8 t. salt

Melt butter with 1/2 teaspoon cinnamon over medium heat in a
10" oven-proof skillet; add apples. Sauté until tender, about 4 minutes;
set aside. Place eggs, apple juice concentrate, flour, half-and-half,
vanilla, remaining cinnamon, nutmeg and salt in a food processor;
process until smooth. Pour over apples; bake at 450 degrees until set,
about 10 minutes. Cut into wedges; place on serving plates. Spoon
apple cream on top before serving. Makes 6 servings.

Apple Cream:

1/2 c. plain yogurt
1/2 t. vanilla extract

2 T. frozen apple juice
    concentrate, thawed

Whisk all ingredients together until smooth.

Having friends over for
breakfast? Set the
table the night
before...one less thing
to think about in
the morning!

Best Brunch Casserole

Lita Hardy
Santa Cruz, CA

My family & friends have been enjoying this dish for over 30 years!

4 c. croutons
2 c. shredded Cheddar cheese
8 eggs, beaten
4 c. milk
1 t. salt

1 t. pepper
2 t. mustard
1 T. dried, minced onion
6 slices bacon, crisply cooked
    and crumbled

Spread croutons in the bottom of a greased 13"x9" baking pan; sprinkle with cheese. Set aside. Whisk eggs, milk, salt, pepper, mustard and onion together; pour over cheese. Sprinkle bacon on top; bake at 325 degrees until set, about 55 to 60 minutes. Serves 8.

Sausage & Egg Muffins

Rhonda Jones
Rocky Mount, VA

Egg-ceptionally easy!

1 lb. ground sausage
1 onion, chopped
12 eggs, beaten
2 c. shredded Cheddar cheese

1 t. garlic powder
1/2 t. salt
1/2 t. pepper

Brown sausage with onion; drain. Combine with remaining ingredients in a large mixing bowl; mix well. Spoon into greased muffin cups, filling 2/3 full; bake at 350 degrees until a knife inserted in the centers removes clean, about 25 minutes. Makes 12 to 15.

Breezy Breakfasts

Raisin-Oat Muffins

Denise Picard
Ventura, CA

*I love making these muffins when friends stop by because I always
have the ingredients on hand.*

1 c. whole-wheat flour
3/4 c. long-cooking oats,
   uncooked
1/2 c. raisins
1/4 c. brown sugar, packed
1 T. baking powder

1/2 t. baking soda
1 t. salt
1/4 t. nutmeg
1 egg, beaten
1 c. milk
1/4 c. oil

Combine the first 8 ingredients in a large mixing bowl; set aside.
Whisk egg, milk and oil together; mix into oat mixture until just
moistened. Fill greased muffin cups half full with batter; bake at
400 degrees until golden, about 20 to 25 minutes. Makes one dozen.

Greet early-morning guests with flowers. Glue a ribbon to
the bottom and up the sides of a tin can, then bring the
ribbon ends up and tie in a bow. Fill the can with water
and several fresh blooms and hang right on the doorknob.

Cappuccino Cooler

*Dianne Gregory
Sheridan, AR*

A perfect pick-me-up drink!

1-1/2 c. prepared coffee, cooled
1-1/2 c. chocolate ice cream,
   softened
1/4 c. chocolate syrup

crushed ice
1 c. frozen whipped topping,
   thawed

Blend coffee, ice cream and syrup together until smooth; set aside.
Fill 4 glasses 3/4 full with ice; add coffee mixture. Top with a spoonful
of whipped topping; serve immediately. Makes 4 servings.

Espresso Whirl

*Patsy Roberts
Center, TX*

*Serve this refreshing drink at brunch or after dinner
in place of dessert.*

1/2 c. prepared espresso, cooled
2 c. milk

1/4 c. sugar
1-1/2 c. crushed ice

Combine all ingredients in a blender; blend well. Pour into chilled
serving glasses; serve immediately. Makes 2 servings.

Offer guests fun toppers for their coffees...vanilla powder, mini chocolate chips, mini marshmallows and whipped topping. Yum!

Breezy Breakfasts

Fabulous Fruit Slush

Pam Klocke
Spicer, MN

An a.m. treat that's sure to delight friends.

1 c. water
1 c. sugar
2 T. lemon juice
12-oz. can frozen orange juice
   concentrate
12-oz. can crushed pineapple,
   drained

17-oz. can fruit cocktail, drained
16-oz. pkg. frozen strawberries,
   thawed and sliced
2 bananas, chopped
6-oz. jar maraschino cherries,
   drained and chopped

Combine water and sugar in a saucepan; heat until sugar is dissolved.
Add lemon and orange juice; heat until completely melted. Remove
from stove; stir in remaining ingredients. Pour mixture into 4 to
6 freezer-proof containers; freeze until solid. Remove containers from
freezer one hour before serving. Makes 4 to 6 servings.

A bowl filled with bright lemons and limes looks so cheery
on a breakfast table...prick them a few times with a fork
to release their delightful scent.

Early-Riser Breakfast

Patty Laughery
Moses Lake, WA

This has become a tradition at Easter and Christmas because it's so easy to prepare the night before and everyone loves it!

8 slices bread, cubed
1 c. shredded Cheddar cheese
1 c. shredded Monterey Jack
   cheese
1-1/2 lbs. ground sausage,
   browned

4 eggs, beaten
3 c. milk, divided
10-3/4 oz. can cream of
   mushroom soup
3/4 t. dry mustard

Arrange bread in an ungreased 13"x9" baking pan; sprinkle with cheeses and sausage. Set aside. Mix eggs and 2-1/2 cups milk together; pour over bread. Cover with aluminum foil; refrigerate overnight. Combine remaining ingredients; pour over bread mixture. Bake, uncovered, at 300 degrees for 1-1/2 hours. Serves 8.

Tiny berry baskets filled with fresh fruit look charming at each place setting. Stick a toothpick through a placecard and prop up inside. Brunch guests will love it!

Breezy Breakfasts

Jump-Start Pizza

Mari MacLean
Bonita, CA

Add your own special toppings before baking.

8-oz. tube refrigerated crescent rolls, separated
28-oz. pkg. frozen shredded hashbrowns with peppers and onions, slightly thawed and divided

6 slices bacon, crisply cooked and crumbled
4-oz. can diced green chiles, drained
1/2 to 1 c. shredded Cheddar cheese
5 eggs, beaten

Arrange crescent rolls to cover the bottom of an ungreased pizza pan; press seams together and pinch edges to form a slight rim. Spread half the hashbrowns evenly over the crust, reserving remaining for another recipe; sprinkle with bacon, chiles and cheese. Carefully pour eggs on top; bake at 375 degrees for 30 to 35 minutes. Slice into wedges to serve. Makes 8 servings.

Surprise overnight guests by leaving special treats in their room...wrap up fragrant soaps in plush terry washcloths, leave a few mints on their pillow or set up a small coffee maker with mugs and individual coffee packets for them to enjoy.

Frozen Fruit Squares

Kristine Marumoto
Sandy, UT

A fresh addition to any breakfast or brunch.

8-oz. pkg. cream cheese,
   softened
1 c. sugar
1-1/2 c. mayonnaise
1 c. chopped pecans
2 bananas, sliced
3 c. frozen whipped topping,
   thawed

2 8-oz. cans crushed
   pineapple, drained
2 10-oz. pkgs. frozen
   strawberries, thawed and
   drained
12-oz. pkg. mini marshmallows
1 c. grapes, halved

Blend cream cheese, sugar and mayonnaise together; fold in remaining ingredients. Spread in an ungreased 13"x9" freezer-safe pan; cover with aluminum foil and freeze. Remove from freezer and allow to soften before cutting into squares. Makes 18 servings.

So fun! Turn Frozen Fruit Squares into circles. Before freezing, spoon mixture into clean 12-ounce juice cans. Once they're frozen, just push fruit mixture from the can and slice into circles.

Breezy Breakfasts

Blueberry-Almond Muffins

Rochelle Sundholm
Eugene, OR

*There's nothing so comforting and delicious as a blueberry muffin
warm from the oven.*

2 c. all-purpose flour
1 T. baking powder
1/4 t. salt
2/3 c. sugar
2 t. lemon zest

1/2 c. milk
1/2 c. butter, melted and cooled
2 eggs
1-1/2 c. blueberries

Combine first 5 ingredients in a large mixing bowl; form a well in
the center. Set aside. Whisk milk, butter and eggs together; pour
into well, stirring until just moistened. Fold in blueberries; fill greased
muffin cups 2/3 full with batter. Sprinkle with topping; bake at
400 degrees for 15 to 20 minutes. Remove from muffin cups
immediately. Makes 20.

Topping:

1/4 c. all-purpose flour
1/4 c. sugar

2 T. chilled butter, sliced
1/3 c. chopped almonds

Combine flour and sugar in a mixing bowl; cut in butter with a pastry
cutter until crumbly. Add almonds; mix well.

Southern Country Casserole

Michelle Garner
Tampa, FL

There won't be any leftovers!

2 c. water
1/2 c. quick-cooking grits,
   uncooked
3-1/2 c. shredded Cheddar
   cheese, divided
4 eggs, beaten

1 c. milk
1/2 t. salt
1/2 t. pepper
1 lb. ground sausage, browned
1 T. fresh parsley, chopped

Bring water to a boil in a large saucepan; add grits. Return to a boil; reduce heat and simmer for 4 minutes. Mix in 2 cups cheese; stir until melted. Remove from heat; add eggs, milk, salt, pepper and sausage, mixing well. Pour into a greased 13"x9" baking pan; bake at 350 degrees for 45 to 50 minutes. Sprinkle with remaining cheese and parsley; return to oven until cheese melts, about 5 minutes. Serves 6 to 8.

Make your gatherings fit your home. Have a tiny dining area but a roomy patio or deck? Plan to invite friends over when you can serve casual meals outdoors.

Breezy Breakfasts

Baked Garden Omelet

Kathy Unruh
Fresno, CA

Here's one omelet you don't have to flip!

8 eggs, beaten
1 c. ricotta cheese
1/2 c. milk
1/2 t. dried basil
1/4 t. salt
1/4 t. fennel seed, crushed
1/4 t. pepper

10-oz. pkg. frozen spinach,
  thawed and drained
1 c. tomatoes, chopped
1 c. shredded mozzarella cheese
1/2 c. green onion, sliced
1/2 c. salami, diced

Whisk eggs and ricotta cheese together in a large mixing bowl; add milk, basil, salt, fennel seed and pepper. Fold in remaining ingredients; spread in a greased 13"x9" baking pan. Bake at 325 degrees until a knife inserted in the center removes clean, about 30 to 35 minutes; let stand 10 minutes before serving. Serves 6 to 8.

Mini Ham Muffins

Linda Stone
Cookville, TN

You can't eat just one!

1 c. self-rising flour
1/4 c. mayonnaise

1/2 c. milk
1 c. cooked ham, chopped

Stir all ingredients together; spoon into greased mini muffin cups. Bake at 350 degrees until golden, about 15 minutes. Makes one dozen.

The ornament of a house is
the friends who frequent it.
- Ralph Waldo Emerson

Crispy French Toast

Kathy Murray-Strunk
Mesa, AZ

This French toast is unlike any I've ever had. It's truly delicious, attractive on a breakfast table and always a favorite.

4 eggs, beaten
1/2 c. milk
1/2 t. cinnamon
1 t. vanilla extract
1/8 t. salt

2 c. corn flake cereal, crushed
1 loaf French bread, cut into
 10 slices
Garnish: maple syrup

Whisk first 5 ingredients together in a shallow dish; set aside. Spread crushed cereal on a plate; set aside. Dip bread slices into egg mixture; turn once to coat both sides. Place in crushed cereal; turn once to coat both sides. Arrange on a buttered baking sheet; bake at 450 degrees for 5 minutes. Flip bread slices; bake 5 additional minutes. Drizzle with syrup; serve warm. Makes 10 servings.

No time to spend on folding napkins? Simply pull each through the hole of a bagel, then set one on each plate...oh-so clever!

Breezy Breakfasts

Gooey Caramel Rolls

Maureen Seidl
Inver Grove Heights, MN

*Years ago I owned a cafe where we perfected this simple recipe.
They can be prepared the day before and cooked the next
morning...just be sure to serve them piping hot!*

1-1/2 c. brown sugar, packed
3/4 c. whipping cream

2 loaves frozen bread dough,
thawed

Whisk brown sugar and whipping cream together; pour into an
ungreased 13"x9" baking pan. Tip to evenly coat bottom; set aside.
Roll out one bread loaf into a 12"x6" rectangle; roll up jelly-roll style
beginning at a short side. Slice into 6, one-inch thick pieces; arrange in
baking pan. Repeat with remaining bread loaf. Cover with plastic
wrap; set aside until dough rises to top of pan. Uncover and bake at
350 degrees for 35 to 45 minutes; let cool slightly. Place a serving
plate tightly over pan; invert to remove rolls. Spoon any remaining
syrup on top; serve warm. Makes one dozen.

A quick & easy breakfast
or brunch
centerpiece...just fill
each muffin cup half
full of coffee
beans, then nestle
a small votive candle in
each. So simple!

Sweet Berry Popover

Elisabeth Macmillan
British Columbia, Canada

Use the freshest berries of the season.

1 c. milk
1 T. butter, melted
1/2 t. vanilla extract
1/4 c. plus 1 T. sugar, divided
1/4 t. salt

1/8 t. nutmeg
1 c. all-purpose flour
2 eggs, beaten
1 c. berries
1/4 t. cinnamon

Whisk milk, butter, vanilla, 1/4 cup sugar, salt and nutmeg together; blend in flour. Gradually mix in eggs; set aside. Butter a 9" pie plate; add berries, leaving a wide border around the rim. Gently pour batter on top; set aside. Combine remaining sugar with cinnamon; sprinkle over the batter. Bake at 450 degrees for 20 minutes; lower heat to 350 degrees without opening the oven door. Continue baking until popover is golden, about 20 additional minutes. Slice into wedges; serve immediately. Makes 8 servings.

Thread cranberries and grapes through wooden skewers and serve with any breakfast beverage...Looks really pretty in orange juice or white grape juice.

Breezy Breakfasts

Strawberry Scones

Jennifer Wickes
Pine Beach, NJ

*I created this recipe after tasting spectacular scones at an
Amish bake sale...these are top-notch!*

2 c. all-purpose flour
1/3 c. sugar
2 t. baking powder
1/4 t. salt
1/3 c. butter
1 egg, beaten

1 t. vanilla extract
1/4 c. whipping cream
1/4 c. buttermilk
1 c. strawberries, hulled and
  sliced
Optional: sugar

Combine flour, sugar, baking powder and salt in a large mixing bowl;
cut in butter with a pastry cutter until coarse crumbs form. Form
a well in the center; set aside. Whisk egg, vanilla, cream and
buttermilk together; stir into dry mixture until just moistened. Fold in
strawberries; gently knead dough on a lightly floured surface until
smooth, about 10 seconds. Pat into a 7-inch circle about one-inch
thick; slice into 8 wedges. Arrange on a parchment paper-lined baking
sheet; brush with glaze and sprinkle with additional sugar, if desired.
Bake at 375 degrees until golden, about 15 minutes. Cool on a wire
rack. Makes 8 servings.

Glaze:

1 egg, beaten

1 T. whipping cream

Whisk egg and cream together.

No-Eggs Breakfast Casserole

Loree Matson
Fort Wayne, IN

A real crowd-pleaser.

30-oz. pkg. frozen shredded
   hashbrowns, thawed
16-oz. container French onion
   dip

1 lb. ground sausage, browned
2 c. sour cream
2 c. shredded Cheddar cheese,
   divided

Combine first 4 ingredients and one cup cheese; mix well. Spread in a greased 13"x9" baking pan; bake at 350 degrees for 45 minutes. Sprinkle with remaining cheese; bake for 15 additional minutes. Serves 4 to 6.

Cheese, Please Pie

Stefan Szabo
Richfield, OH

Try stirring in diced sun-dried tomatoes, red pepper or green chiles.

1 egg
3/4 c. all-purpose flour
1/2 t. garlic salt

pepper to taste
1 c. milk, divided
1 c. shredded Muenster cheese

Whisk egg, flour, garlic salt, pepper and 1/2 cup milk together until smooth; gradually blend in remaining milk. Stir in cheese; pour into a greased 9" glass pie plate. Bake at 425 degrees until puffed and set, about 25 to 30 minutes. Cut into wedges; serve warm. Serves 4.

All happiness depends on a leisurely breakfast.
– John Gunther

Breezy Breakfasts

Chef's Baked Oatmeal

Laura Leeper
Altoona, IA

A yummy way to warm up tummies on chilly mornings.

3 c. quick-cooking oats,
   uncooked
2 t. baking powder
1 t. salt

1/2 c. butter, softened
2 eggs
2 c. milk

Stir together oats, baking powder and salt in a mixing bowl; set aside. In a separate bowl, combine butter, eggs and milk; blend into dry ingredients. Pour into an ungreased 13"x9" baking pan; bake at 375 degrees for 25 minutes. Serves 6 to 8.

Top off each bowl of Chef's Baked Oatmeal with a dainty edible flower...they add eye-catching color along with a delightful flavor. Grow them yourself or look for pesticide-free blooms in the supermarket. For a sweet taste, try roses, squash blossoms, daylilies or violets.

Sweet Apple Rolls

Mary Morrison
Zanoni, MO

I like to use gooseberries, strawberries and rhubarb too!

2 c. all-purpose flour
3/4 c. shortening
2-1/2 c. water, divided

5 apples, cored, peeled and
    chopped
2 c. sugar
1/2 c. margarine

Mix flour and shortening together; stir in 1/2 cup water. Roll out into
1/2-inch thick rectangle; sprinkle with apples. Roll up jelly-roll style;
cut into twelve slices. Arrange in an ungreased 13"x9" baking pan; set
aside. Combine remaining water, sugar and margarine in a saucepan;
heat until sugar is dissolved. Pour over rolls; bake at 350 degrees for
50 minutes. Makes one dozen.

Puffy Pancakes

Stephanie Herrel
Oswego, IL

Cut into squares and drizzle your favorite syrup over top.

1/2 c. butter
1 c. milk
1 c. all-purpose flour

4 eggs, beaten
Garnish: powdered sugar

Place butter in a 13"x9" baking pan; heat in a 425-degree oven until
melted. Whisk remaining ingredients together; pour over butter,
without mixing. Bake at 425 degrees for 20 minutes; sprinkle with
powdered sugar before serving. Makes 8 to 10 servings.

Lay pancakes on a baking sheet and place in a low oven to
keep warm until all the batter is used.

Breezy Breakfasts

Pear Pancake
Jo Ann

Top each slice with a sprinkling of powdered sugar...yum!

4 pears, cored, peeled and sliced
1/4 c. brown sugar, packed
1/4 c. lemon juice
1 c. all-purpose flour
1 c. milk

3 T. sugar
1 t. vanilla extract
1/4 t. salt
3 eggs, beaten

Combine pears, brown sugar and lemon juice; stir well. Pour into a 12" skillet; sauté until pears are golden, about 5 minutes. Remove from heat; set aside. Place flour in a large mixing bowl; set aside. Whisk remaining ingredients together; pour into flour, mix well. Pour batter into an ungreased 12" oven-proof skillet; bake at 425 degrees until golden and puffy, about 25 minutes. Spoon warm pear mixture into the center before serving. Serves 4.

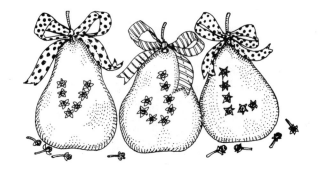

Add a simple, yet elegant touch to a brunch with friends. Stick whole cloves into firm pears to spell the first initial of each guest's name. Tie a sheer ribbon around each stem and stand the pears up at place settings.

Get Up & Go Granola

Nicole Shira
New Baltimore, MI

Sprinkle over yogurt for a satisfying breakfast treat.

zest of 2 oranges
1/3 c. maple syrup
1/2 c. oil
4 c. quick-cooking oats,
   uncooked
1 c. sliced almonds
2 c. mixed nuts

1/8 t. salt
1/3 c. honey
2-1/2 t. cinnamon
1/2 t. nutmeg
3/4 c. chopped dried apricots
3/4 c. chopped dried cherries
2 c. flaked coconut, toasted

Mix orange zest, maple syrup and oil together in a heavy saucepan; bring to a boil. Boil for one minute; remove from heat. Stir in oats, almonds, nuts, salt, honey, cinnamon, nutmeg, apricots and cherries; spread onto an ungreased baking sheet. Bake at 350 degrees for 10 to 15 minutes; remove from oven. Sprinkle with coconut; cool. Break into pieces; store in an airtight container. Makes 10 cups.

Create a cereal station for a quick & easy breakfast. Set out 3 to 4 different kinds of cereal, Get Up & Go Granola and pitchers of ice cold milk. Add a bowl of fresh fruit to the spread along with O.J., coffee and hot cocoa. You can even prepare oatmeal and keep it on the stove for guests to serve themselves.

Breezy Breakfasts

Fruity Oatmeal Coffee Cake

Natalie Holdren
Topeka, KS

Best served with an icy glass of milk!

1 c. whole-wheat flour
3/4 t. baking powder
1/2 t. allspice
1-1/2 c. quick-cooking oats,
    uncooked and divided
1 c. brown sugar, packed and
    divided
1/2 t. salt
1/2 t. cinnamon

2 t. vanilla extract
1 egg
1/2 c. chopped nuts
1/2 c. raisins
1 c. strawberries, hulled and
    chopped
1 banana, sliced
1/4 c. margarine

Combine flour, baking powder, allspice, one cup oats, 3/4 cup brown sugar, salt and cinnamon; stir in vanilla, egg, nuts, raisins, strawberries and banana. Spoon into a greased 9"x9" baking pan; set aside. Mix remaining oats and brown sugar together; cut in margarine until crumbly. Sprinkle over fruit mixture; bake at 350 degrees for 35 minutes. Makes 9 servings.

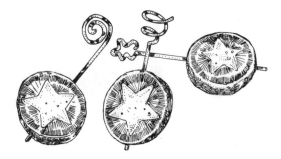

Bite-size beauties! Slice kiwi into 1/4-inch thick slices, then use a cookie cutter to cut out star shapes from the middle. Cut stars from melon slices, and fit the melon star into the opening in the kiwi.

Whole-Grain Jam Squares

Ellen Gibson
Orlando, FL

Stack on a jadite plate before serving...so pretty!

2 c. quick-cooking oats,
   uncooked
1-3/4 c. all-purpose flour
3/4 t. salt
1/2 t. baking soda

1 c. butter
1 c. brown sugar, packed
1/2 c. chopped walnuts
1 t. cinnamon
3/4 to 1 c. strawberry preserves

Combine the first 8 ingredients in a mixing bowl; stir until crumbly. Place 2 cups mixture to the side; press remaining mixture into the bottom of a greased 13"x9" baking pan. Spread preserves over the top; sprinkle with remaining oat mixture. Bake at 400 degrees for 25 to 30 minutes or until golden; cool. Cut into squares. Makes 2 dozen.

Butterscotch Banana Bread

Claire McGeough
Lebanon, NJ

My husband's favorite breakfast treat.

3-1/2 c. all-purpose flour
4 t. baking powder
1 t. baking soda
1 t. cinnamon
1 t. nutmeg
2 c. bananas, mashed

1-1/2 c. sugar
2 eggs
1/2 c. butter, melted
1/2 c. milk
12-oz. pkg. butterscotch chips,
   melted

Combine the first 6 ingredients together; set aside. Blend sugar, eggs and butter together in a large mixing bowl; gradually add flour mixture alternately with milk, mixing well. Fold in butterscotch chips; pour batter equally into 2 greased and floured 9"x5" loaf pans. Bake at 350 degrees for 60 to 70 minutes. Cool 15 minutes; remove from pans. Serve warm or cold. Makes 16 servings.

Breezy Breakfasts

Cinnamon-Apple Pancakes

Stephanie Moon
Silverdale, WA

Light and fluffy!

2 c. all-purpose flour
1 t. baking soda
2 t. baking powder
1 T. brown sugar, packed
1 t. salt
1 t. cinnamon

2 eggs
1-1/2 c. buttermilk
1/2 c. sour cream
1/4 c. margarine, melted
1 apple, cored, peeled and grated

Combine flour, baking soda, baking powder, brown sugar, salt and cinnamon in a large mixing bowl; set aside. Mix eggs, buttermilk, sour cream and margarine together; add to flour mixture. Fold in apple; pour 1/4 cup batter onto a greased hot griddle. Heat until golden on both sides, turning once. Serves 4 to 6.

Fun shapes for everyone! Spoon pancake batter into a plastic zipping bag, snip off one corner and gently squeeze batter onto a hot griddle into any shape...make cute animal shapes or alphabet letters.

3-Ingredient Sausage Squares

Shelley Wellington
Dyersburg, TN

This recipe can easily be halved and baked in an 8"x8" pan.

2 lbs. ground sausage
2 8-oz. pkgs. cream cheese, softened

2 8-oz. tubes refrigerated crescent rolls

Brown sausage in a 12" skillet; drain. Add cream cheese, stirring until melted and well blended; remove from heat and set aside. Press dough from one tube crescent rolls in a greased 13"x9" baking pan, being sure to cover bottom and part way up sides of pan; press perforations together. Pour sausage mixture over top; set aside. Roll remaining crescent roll dough into a 13"x9" rectangle; layer over sausage mixture. Bake at 350 degrees for 15 to 20 minutes or until golden; cut into squares to serve. Serves 6 to 8.

Zucchini Quiche

Rosemarie Rizzo
Toms River, NJ

Always a favorite!

4 eggs, beaten
1/4 c. grated Parmesan cheese
1/4 c. shredded mozzarella cheese
1/2 c. oil

1 c. biscuit baking mix
3 c. zucchini, thinly sliced
1/2 onion, chopped
1 t. fresh parsley, minced
1 t. garlic powder

Combine the first 5 ingredients; blend until smooth. Add remaining ingredients; stir well. Spread in a lightly greased 9" pie plate; bake at 350 degrees for 30 minutes. Makes 8 servings.

Breezy Breakfasts

Crustless Swiss Broccoli Quiche

Terri Dillingham
Windsor, NY

Serve with buttery toast.

4 eggs
3 T. all-purpose flour
1/2 t. dried oregano
1/8 t. pepper
1-1/2 c. milk
2 c. shredded Swiss cheese

1/4 c. green onion, sliced
10-oz. pkg. frozen chopped
   broccoli, partially thawed
1/4 c. olives with pimentos,
   sliced

Blend first 5 ingredients together; gradually stir in the remaining ingredients. Pour into an ungreased 9" pie plate; bake at 350 degrees for 45 to 50 minutes. Makes 8 servings.

Make 'em mini! Bake Zucchini Quiche or
Crustless Swiss Broccoli Quiche in mini muffin cups for
individual servings...just decrease baking time by
10 minutes. Top each with a dainty dollop of sour cream
and a sprig of dill. So pretty!

Blueberry Pillows

Kristie Rigo
Friedens, PA

A delightful blend of cream cheese and blueberries stuffed inside French toast.

8-oz. pkg. cream cheese,
   softened
16 slices Italian bread
1/2 c. blueberries

2 eggs
1/2 c. milk
1 t. vanilla extract

Spread cream cheese evenly on 8 bread slices; arrange blueberries evenly over the cream cheese. Top with remaining bread slices, gently pressing to seal; set aside. Whisk eggs, milk and vanilla together in a shallow dish; brush over bread slices. Arrange on a hot griddle; heat until golden. Flip and heat other side until golden. Serves 8.

Sticky Buns

*Catherine Smith
Champlin, MN*

A quick & easy way to welcome morning guests.

18 frozen dinner rolls
3-1/2 oz. pkg. cook & serve
   butterscotch pudding mix

1/2 c. butter, melted
1/2 c. brown sugar, packed
1 t. cinnamon

Place rolls in a greased Bundt® pan; sprinkle with pudding mix. Set aside. Combine butter, brown sugar and cinnamon; pour over rolls. Cover tightly with buttered aluminum foil; let rise overnight. Uncover and bake at 350 degrees for 30 to 40 minutes; carefully invert onto a serving platter. Makes 18 servings.

Appetizers
1~2~3

Toasted Almond Party Spread

Karen Sweitzer
Columbus, OH

Delicious with assorted crackers and savory bread rounds.

8-oz. pkg. cream cheese,
  softened
1-1/2 c. shredded Swiss cheese
1/3 c. mayonnaise

2 T. green onion, chopped
1/8 t. nutmeg
1/8 t. pepper
1/3 c. sliced almonds, toasted

Combine all ingredients; mix well. Spread in an ungreased 9" pie plate; bake at 350 degrees for 15 minutes. Serves 6.

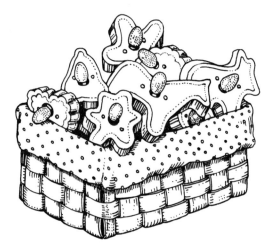

Use mini cookie cutters to cut toasted bread
into charming shapes to serve alongside
savory dips and spreads.

Appetizers 1~2~3

Brie with Caramelized Onions

Kathleen Richter
Bridgeport, CT

Topped with cranberries and pistachios, this Brie is a hit at any holiday gathering. Serve with baguette slices for a very simple yet elegant appetizer.

5-oz. wheel Brie cheese
1 onion, chopped
2 T. butter
1/2 c. brown sugar, packed

1/2 c. dried cranberries
2 T. balsamic vinegar
1/4 c. chopped pistachios

Place Brie in a greased 9" pie plate; bake at 350 degrees for 10 minutes. Remove from oven; set aside. Sauté onion in butter until tender, about 5 minutes; add brown sugar, cranberries and vinegar. Heat until mixture caramelizes and thickens, about 5 minutes; pour over Brie. Sprinkle with pistachios; serve warm. Serves 6.

Group a selection of appetizers on a small table separate from the main serving tables so early-comers can nibble while the rest of the crowd gathers.

Cream Cheese Terrine

Amy Palsrok
Silverdale, WA

This is also known as $20 dip to my friends & family because it looks (and tastes!) like it's from a gourmet store. Serve with shaped crackers for the most impressive display.

4 8-oz. pkgs. cream cheese,
   softened and divided
2 cloves garlic
1/8 t. dried basil, chopped
7-oz. pkg. sun-dried tomatoes

3 T. green onion, sliced
1/8 t. dried parsley
4-oz. pkg. crumbled blue cheese
1/2 c. sliced almonds
7-oz. jar basil pesto

Combine first package cream cheese and garlic; spread into a plastic wrap-lined 8"x4" loaf pan. Sprinkle with basil; set aside. Mix second package cream cheese with tomatoes and green onion; spread over first layer. Sprinkle with parsley; set aside. Stir third package cream cheese with blue cheese and almonds; spread over tomato layer. Set aside. Combine remaining package cream cheese and pesto; spread over blue cheese mixture. Cover and refrigerate for at least one hour; remove to serving platter by gently pulling up on plastic wrap, invert onto platter and peel away plastic wrap. Serves 12.

When serving appetizers, a good rule of thumb for quantities is 6 to 8 per person if dinner will follow and 12 to 15 per person if it's an appetizer-only gathering.

Appetizers 1~2~3

Crab-Stuffed Mushrooms

Cindy Skinner
Hagerstown, MD

Your friends will think you spent the whole day in the kitchen!

15 mushrooms, stems removed
   and reserved
1 slice bread, crumbled
7-oz. can crabmeat, drained
salt and pepper to taste
1 egg, beaten
1/2 t. seafood seasoning
1/3 c. onion, chopped
Garnish: grated Parmesan
   cheese
2 T. butter, melted

Chop mushroom stems; combine with bread crumbs, crabmeat, salt, pepper, egg, seafood seasoning and onion. Mix well; spoon into mushroom caps. Sprinkle with Parmesan cheese; set aside. Coat bottom of a 13"x9" baking pan with butter; arrange mushroom caps on top. Broil for 2 to 4 minutes or until heated through and golden. Makes 15.

Add some sparkle to the table! Wrap inexpensive beaded bracelets around old canning jars. Set a tea light inside each jar or add simple arrangements of flowers. Guests can even take them home as favors.

Cucumber Canapés

Dawn Pryor
Jefferson, MD

*These are a favorite of my friends, family and co-workers. The fresh
dill and chives combine for a distinct and refreshing flavor.*

1 c. mayonnaise
3-oz. pkg. cream cheese,
   softened
1 T. onion, grated
1 T. fresh chives, minced
1/2 c. vinegar

1/2 c. Worcestershire sauce
1/8 t. garlic powder
1/8 t. dried parsley
1/8 t. fresh dill, chopped
1 to 2 baguettes, thinly sliced
2 cucumbers, sliced

Combine the first 9 ingredients together in a blender; blend until
smooth. Cover; refrigerate for 24 hours. Spread on bread slices; top
with a cucumber slice. Makes about 4 dozen.

To give cucumber slices a decorated edge, draw the tines
of a fork lengthwise down the side of a whole cucumber,
making grooves about 1/16-inch deep. Continue around
the cucumber, then cut into slices.

Appetizers 1~2~3

Delicious Dill Dip

Paula Dreessen
Merriam, KS

Serve in a round of pumpernickel bread...scoop out the inside and use for dipping!

8-oz. pkg. cream cheese,
  softened
1 c. sour cream
1 c. mayonnaise

1/2 c. green onion, chopped
2-1/4 oz. can sliced black olives,
  drained
1 T. dill weed

Blend together until smooth. Serves 6 to 8.

Turn ordinary cherry tomatoes into party favorites. Cut off the top of each tomato, scoop out the seeds with a small melon baller and turn over to drain on paper towels. Pipe Delicious Dill Dip (or softened cream cheese) into hollowed tomatoes and sprinkle fresh dill over top.

Stuffed Jalapeños

Karen McGrady
Worthington, PA

Cool down these cheese-stuffed peppers by dipping them in sour cream.

8-oz. pkg. cream cheese, softened
1 c. shredded Cheddar cheese
1 c. mayonnaise
1 clove garlic, minced

18 jalapeños, halved
1 egg white
1 T. milk
1 c. corn flake cereal, crushed

Mix cream cheese, Cheddar cheese, mayonnaise and garlic together; spoon into jalapeños. Set aside. Combine egg white and milk; roll each jalapeño in egg white mixture. Coat with crushed cereal; arrange on an ungreased baking sheet. Bake at 375 degrees for 15 minutes. Makes 36.

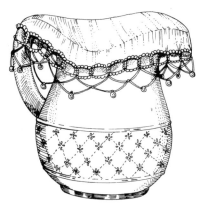

Platters of food set on different levels make a more interesting presentation. Use books, a stack of plates or upside-down pots and bowls on a buffet table to create different heights, cover with a tablecloth and set serving dishes on top!

Appetizers 1~2~3

Festive Chicken Enchilada Dip

Jeannine English
Wylie, TX

Terrific served with crispy corn tortilla chips.

2 8-oz. pkgs. cream cheese,
   softened
1-1/3 c. shredded Cheddar
   cheese
1 t. minced garlic
1-1/2 T. chili powder
1 t. cumin
1 t. dried oregano

1 t. paprika
cayenne pepper to taste
3 boneless, skinless chicken
   breasts, cooked and chopped
1 bunch cilantro, chopped
4 green onions, chopped
10-oz. can diced tomatoes with
   green chiles

Mix cheeses together until well blended; add garlic, chili powder,
cumin, oregano, paprika and cayenne pepper. Mix well; stir in
remaining ingredients. Cover and refrigerate overnight. Serves 12.

A new way to serve Festive Chicken Enchilada Dip! Just
spread dip onto flour tortillas, roll up jelly-roll style
and cut into one-inch slices....add some kick by
topping each with a jalapeño pepper slice.

30-Minute Olive Appetizer

*Joanne Walker
Ontario, Canada*

*Freeze baked squares until ready to use, then just heat up in the
microwave...so easy!*

8-oz. tube refrigerated crescent
   rolls
2 eggs, beaten
1 c. shredded Cheddar cheese

1/2 c. onion, minced
3 T. butter, softened
1 c. olives with pimentos, sliced

Spread crescent rolls to cover the bottom of a greased 13"x9" baking
pan; set aside. Mix remaining ingredients together; spread over
crust. Bake at 350 degrees for 15 to 20 minutes; cut into bite-size
squares. Makes 4 dozen.

Here's a fun way to invite guests over:
Fill bouquets of balloons with helium and write the who,
what and where party information on each with a
permanent pen. Hand deliver or tie securely to doorknobs
with lengths of curling ribbon.

Appetizers 1-2-3

Denise's Meatballs

Audra Webb
Halifax, VA

*I first tasted these delicious meatballs at a family Christmas party.
They are so simple to make and are absolutely wonderful
any time of the year!*

3 lbs. ground beef
12-oz. can evaporated milk
1 c. quick-cooking oats,
   uncooked
1 c. crackers, crushed
2 eggs

1/2 c. onion, chopped
1/2 t. garlic salt
2 t. salt
1/2 t. pepper
2 t. chili powder

Combine all ingredients together, mixing thoroughly. Shape into
one-inch round balls; arrange in an ungreased 13"x9" baking pan.
Cover with sauce; bake at 350 degrees for one hour, basting
occasionally. Serves 15.

Sauce:

2 c. catsup
1 c. brown sugar, packed
1/2 t. liquid smoke

1/2 t. garlic salt
1/4 c. onion, chopped

Combine all ingredients; mix well.

Dining is and always was a great
artistic opportunity.
- Frank Lloyd Wright

Creamy Crab Dip

Regina Spencer
Olympia, WA

A delicious spread for toasted mini bagels.

1 c. mayonnaise-type salad
   dressing
8-oz. pkg. cream cheese,
   softened
2 T. lemon juice
1 stalk celery, chopped

8-oz. can crabmeat, drained and
   chopped
3 green onions, chopped
8-oz. can water chestnuts,
   drained and chopped

Blend salad dressing and cream cheese together until smooth and creamy; stir in remaining ingredients. Cover and refrigerate until firm. Makes 4 cups.

Guests will love these dippers. Thread carrot and celery slices, cauliflower and broccoli flowerets and olives onto small wooden skewers in different combinations...arrange around yummy dips and enjoy!

Appetizers 1~2~3

Slam-Dunk Vegetable Dip

Irene Putman
Canal Fulton, OH

This dip has been enjoyed at all kinds of events over the past 30 years...everyone always raves about it and asks for the recipe. My husband likes to use it as a condiment on sandwiches too!

2 c. mayonnaise
1/4 c. onion, chopped
3/4 t. paprika
3/4 t. Worcestershire sauce

1 t. prepared horseradish
8 drops hot pepper sauce
1/2 t. dry mustard
1/2 t. curry powder

Mix all ingredients together; chill. Makes about 2 cups.

Family Chip Dip

Geraldine Sherwood
Schererville, IN

Someone always volunteers to bring this to our family get-togethers. If it is ever forgotten, we'll go buy the ingredients and whip it up right then and there...it's a must-have!

8-oz. pkg. cream cheese,
   softened
1/3 c. catsup
1 T. milk

2 T. French salad dressing
2 t. Worcestershire sauce
1 onion, minced

Combine all ingredients together in a mixing bowl; blend until smooth and creamy. Makes about 1-1/2 cups.

So-Simple Hummus

Anne Girucky
Norfolk, VA

Serve with sliced pita rounds...it couldn't be easier!

15-1/2 oz. can chickpeas,
   drained
1 clove garlic, minced

1 T. olive oil
1 to 2 T. tahini paste or sesame
   seed paste

Combine chickpeas and garlic in a food processor; process until smooth. Gradually add remaining ingredients; blending until creamy. Makes 2 cups.

Dress up paper napkins in a snap! Trim napkin edges with decorative-edge scissors, then use permanent markers and rubber stamps to add polka dots, stripes or alphabet letters.

Appetizers 1-2-3

Pesto Packages

Jennifer Rudolph
Oakley, CA

For a bite-size snack...slice each crescent roll into 2 triangles before adding cheese and sauce.

Brie cheese, sliced
8-oz. tube refrigerated crescent
  rolls, separated

7-oz. jar pesto sauce

Place one slice Brie in the center of each crescent roll; spoon pesto sauce on top. Roll up crescents; pinch seams closed. Arrange on an ungreased baking sheet; bake according to crescent roll package directions. Makes 8.

Fresh Pesto Spread

Carol Burns
Delaware, OH

Spread over bread slices and broil until golden.

1/2 c. fresh basil, loosely packed
2 t. olive oil
1 t. lemon juice
1 clove garlic, minced

1 T. pine nuts
2 T. cold water
1 T. grated Parmesan cheese

Combine all ingredients except Parmesan cheese in a blender; pulse until smooth. Spoon into a glass bowl; stir in Parmesan cheese. Makes about 1/3 cup.

Keep a folder or drawer for clippings from magazines and newspapers...Look for easy recipes, fun menus and party ideas you'd like to try.

Party Cheese Ball

Sarah Sommers
Atwater, CA

Everyone will be going back for more so be sure to have plenty of crackers...it's simply addicting!

2 8-oz. pkgs. cream cheese,
   softened
2 c. shredded sharp Cheddar
   cheese
1 t. pimento, chopped
1 t. onion, minced
1 t. lemon juice

1 t. green pepper, chopped
2 t. Worcestershire sauce
1/8 t. cayenne pepper
1/8 t. salt
Garnish: chopped pecans and
   fresh parsley, minced

Blend cream cheese until light and fluffy; add Cheddar cheese, pimento, onion, lemon juice, green pepper, Worcestershire sauce, pepper and salt. Shape into a ball; wrap in plastic wrap and refrigerate until firm. Roll in pecans and parsley. Serves 12 to 16.

Single servings! Roll Party Cheese Ball into mini balls and place in paper muffin cups. Fill more paper muffin cups with crackers and pretzels and arrange alongside mini cheese balls...guests can enjoy one of each!

Appetizers 1~2~3

Pepper-Swiss Cheese Log

Gail Prather
Isanti, MN

A big hit with any crowd!

2 3-oz. pkgs. cream cheese,
   softened
1/2 c. sour cream
1/4 t. garlic salt

1-1/2 c. shredded Swiss cheese
2 T. fresh parsley, minced
2 to 3 T. pepper

Blend cream cheese until smooth; add sour cream and garlic salt. Mix in Swiss cheese and parsley; cover and refrigerate for at least 2 hours. Shape into a log; sprinkle with pepper. Serves 8.

Jazzed-Up Cream Cheese Ball

Susie Kadleck
San Antonio, TX

A classic appetizer that's so easy to make.

3 8-oz. pkgs. cream cheese,
   softened
1 green pepper, chopped
8-oz. can crushed pineapple,
   drained

1 T. garlic salt
1 T. onion, minced
1 T. seasoned salt
1-1/2 c. chopped pecans

Combine first 6 ingredients together; mix well. Shape into a ball; roll in pecans. Wrap in plastic wrap; refrigerate until firm. Serves 18.

Creamy Artichoke-Garlic Dip

Jackie Smulski
Lyons, IL

We like it best with veggies and pita chips.

16-oz. jar marinated artichoke
   hearts, drained
2 T. fresh parsley, chopped
2 cloves garlic, minced
2 T. lemon juice

1-1/4 c. sour cream
1/4 c. mayonnaise
1/8 t. pepper
1/8 t. cayenne pepper

Place the first 4 ingredients in a food processor; process until smooth.
Add remaining ingredients; process until well blended. Cover and
refrigerate overnight. Makes about 3-1/2 cups.

Create quick chip 'n dip sets in no time. Spoon dips into
pottery soup bowls and set each bowl on top of
dinner plates which hold crackers, veggies,
pretzels, chips and bread.

Appetizers 1~2~3

Baked Artichoke-Spinach Spread

Kelly Francis
Encino, CA

Serve with fresh French bread slices...delicious!

1 c. mayonnaise
1 c. shredded Parmesan cheese
16-oz. jar non-marinated
  artichoke hearts, drained
  and mashed

10-oz. pkg. frozen chopped
  spinach, thawed and drained
minced garlic to taste

Combine all ingredients; mix well. Spread in an ungreased 9" pie plate. Bake at 350 degrees until bubbly, about 40 minutes. Serves 8.

Add some whimsy to a wintertime gathering. Before guests arrive, fill a punch bowl with clean, fresh snow and nestle glasses inside to chill. Guests can grab a glass and fill with soda or punch...it's sure to stay extra cool!

Sweet Salsa

Traci Doxtator
Henderson, NV

My friend Marcia and I have had such fun entertaining each other's families every weekend...and we've built the most special friendship over salsa, chips and a deck of cards!

2 c. cantaloupe, peeled and
    finely chopped
2 c. cherry tomatoes, chopped
1/4 c. green onion, chopped
1/4 c. fresh basil, chopped

2 T. jalapeños, diced
2 T. lime juice
2 T. orange juice
1/4 t. salt
1/8 t. pepper

Stir all ingredients together; cover and refrigerate for at least 30 minutes. Makes about 4-3/4 cups.

Make your own tortilla chips to go with homemade salsas and dips...you won't believe how easy it is. Just slice flour tortillas into wedges, spray with non-stick vegetable spray and bake at 350 degrees for 5 to 7 minutes.

Appetizers 1-2-3

Black Bean Salsa

Remona Putman
Rockwood, PA

Excellent with chips or rolled up in flour tortillas.

16-oz. can black beans, rinsed
   and drained
7-oz. can corn, drained
2 cloves garlic, minced
1/2 c. Italian salad dressing
1/2 t. hot pepper sauce

3/4 t. chili powder
3 T. fresh cilantro, chopped
1 tomato, chopped
1/2 sweet onion, chopped
1/2 green pepper, chopped

Combine the first 7 ingredients; cover and refrigerate for 4 to 5 hours. Add remaining ingredients before serving; toss gently. Makes about 5 cups.

Easy Slow-Cooker Bean Dip

Marni Senner
Long Beach, CA

So easy to tote to potlucks and family gatherings.

4 16-oz. cans refried beans
1-lb. pkg. Colby Jack cheese,
   cubed
1-1/4 oz. pkg. taco seasoning
   mix

1 bunch green onions, chopped
1 c. sour cream
8-oz. pkg. cream cheese, cubed

Place all ingredients in a slow cooker; stir to mix. Heat on low setting until cheeses melt, about 2 to 3 hours. Stir often. Serves 12.

Everyone's Favorite Party Mix

Jennie Wiseman
Coshocton, OH

I like to package this mix in tins to hand out to family & friends...the empty tins often make their way back to me to be refilled!

5 c. doughnut-shaped oat cereal
5 c. bite-size crispy corn or rice cereal squares
9.4-oz. pkg. candy-coated chocolates

12-oz. jar peanuts
15-oz. pkg. mini pretzels
2 12-oz. pkgs. white chocolate chips
3 T. oil

Combine the first 5 ingredients in a large roasting pan; set aside. Place the chocolate chips and oil in a microwave-safe bowl; heat until melted, stirring often. Pour over cereal mixture; toss to coat. Spread mix on wax paper; let dry until firm. Break into pieces; store in an airtight container. Makes 20 servings.

For a cozy centerpiece, place a hurricane candle in the middle of the table, then surround it with small glass bowls filled with Everyone's Favorite Party Mix...the candlelight will make the treat bowls sparkle!

Appetizers 1~2~3

Sweet-Tooth Cheese Ball

Joy Diomede
Double Oak, TX

Unbeatable when served with chocolate graham crackers and vanilla wafers.

8-oz. pkg. cream cheese, softened
1/2 c. butter, softened
1/4 t. vanilla extract

2 T. brown sugar, packed
3/4 c. powdered sugar
3/4 c. mini chocolate chips
3/4 c. chopped pecans

Blend cream cheese, butter and vanilla together until fluffy; gradually mix in sugars. Fold in chocolate chips and pecans; wrap in plastic wrap. Refrigerate for at least 2 hours before serving. Serves 8.

Fluffy Peanut Butter Dip

Louise Grant
Glendale, AZ

Serve with a platter piled high with fresh fruits.

1/2 c. creamy peanut butter
8-oz. container vanilla yogurt
1/8 t. cinnamon

1/2 c. frozen whipped topping, thawed

Mix the first 3 ingredients together; stir in whipped topping. Makes 2 cups.

Instead of serving all the food in one room, try using different rooms throughout the house for entertaining...set up one for appetizers, one for dinner and one to serve coffee and desserts.

Spicy Buffalo Bites

Andrew Burns
Norwich, OH

Serve with additional hot sauce for those who really want to turn up the heat!

3/4 c. cooked chicken, shredded
4 t. hot pepper sauce
2 T. Dijon mustard
36 herb-flavored shredded
   wheat crackers

2 T. margarine, melted
4-oz. pkg. crumbled blue cheese
2 T. celery, minced

Combine first 3 ingredients together; mix well. Place one teaspoon mixture on each cracker; drizzle with margarine. Stir crumbled blue cheese and celery together; spread over chicken mixture. Arrange on ungreased baking sheets; bake at 400 degrees until cheese melts, about 4 minutes. Makes 3 dozen.

Honey-Glazed Chicken Wings

Janet McRoberts
Lexington, KY

A zippy appetizer just right for hungry teenagers!

12 chicken wings
1/2 c. barbecue sauce

1/2 c. honey
1/2 c. soy sauce

Arrange chicken wings in a greased 13"x9" baking pan; set aside. Whisk remaining ingredients together; pour over wings. Bake at 350 degrees for 50 to 60 minutes or until juices run clear when chicken is pierced with a fork. Serves 4.

Appetizers 1-2-3

Aloha Chicken Wings

Dianne Gregory
Sheridan, AR

A staple at summer cookouts and backyard gatherings.

1/4 c. butter
1/2 c. catsup
1 clove garlic, minced
3 lbs. chicken wings
1 c. bread crumbs

14-oz. can pineapple chunks,
  juice reserved
2 T. brown sugar, packed
1 T. whole ginger, minced
1 T. Worcestershire sauce
hot pepper sauce to taste

Place butter in a jelly-roll pan; heat in a 400-degree oven until melted. Stir catsup and garlic together; brush over wings. Coat with bread crumbs; arrange in jelly-roll pan, turning to coat both sides with melted butter. Bake at 400 degrees for 30 minutes. While baking, drain pineapple juice; place pineapple chunks to the side and reserve juice. Add enough water to juice to equal 3/4 cup liquid; pour into a small mixing bowl. Whisk in remaining ingredients; pour over wings. Continue baking until juices run clear when chicken is pierced with a fork, about 20 to 30 additional minutes; place pineapple around wings, baking until heated through. Serves 4.

Hosting a backyard gathering? Fill a wheelbarrow or a child's wagon with ice and tuck in bottles of soda and lemonade. Use colorful ribbon to tie a bottle opener to the handle so it stays near the drinks.

Baked Onion Dip

Debi DeVore
Dover, OH

Serve with a fun assortment of pretzels...rods, twists, bits and waffles.

1 c. mayonnaise
1 c. onion, chopped
1 T. grated Parmesan cheese

1/4 t. garlic salt
1 c. shredded Swiss cheese

Combine all ingredients; spread in an ungreased one-quart casserole dish. Bake at 350 degrees for 40 minutes. Makes about 3 cups.

Sausage-Cheese Dip

Margie Williams
Gooseberry Patch

Always a hit on those crisp, football tailgating days!

1 lb. ground beef
1 lb. ground sausage
1 t. cumin

2-lb. pkg. Mexican pasteurized processed cheese spread, cubed

Brown beef and sausage with cumin; drain. Place in a slow cooker; add cheese. Heat on low setting until cheese melts, about 2 to 3 hours. Serves 12.

Fill different baskets with dippers like pretzels, bagel chips, veggies, bread cubes and potato chips. Use a small riser (a book works well) to set under one side of the bottom of each basket to create a tilt...looks so nice and guests can grab dippers easily!

Appetizers 1-2-3

Flaky Sausage Wraps

Carmen Clever
Ashland, OH

Two of these hearty appetizers makes a meal!

6-oz. pkg. ground sausage
1/4 c. onion, chopped
1/4 c. green pepper, chopped
1 clove garlic, minced
1/4 t. mustard

3-oz. pkg. cream cheese,
  softened
1 T. green onion, chopped
8-oz. tube refrigerated crescent
  rolls, separated

Brown sausage with onion, green pepper and garlic; drain. Reduce heat; add mustard, cream cheese and onion, stirring until cheese melts. Cool slightly; place in a food processor. Process until smooth; spread on crescent rolls. Roll up crescent-roll style; arrange on an ungreased baking sheet. Bake at 350 degrees for 10 to 12 minutes. Makes 8.

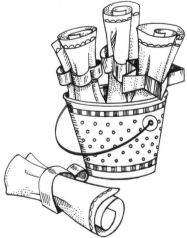

Designate a drawer or a shelf for keeping all the little things you usually have to hunt down when expecting guests. Be sure to include matches, toothpicks, a corkscrew, coffee filters and birthday candles...you'll be glad you thought ahead!

Strawberry-Tea Punch

Vickie

Try making a batch using raspberries instead of strawberries too...it's just as tasty!

6-oz. can lemonade concentrate, partially thawed
1/2 c. sugar
1 t. vanilla extract

1 pt. strawberries, hulled and sliced
2 qts. brewed tea, cooled
ice cubes

Blend lemonade concentrate, sugar, vanilla and strawberries together; pour into tea, stirring well. Pour over ice cubes in serving glasses. Serves 10.

A sweet gesture! Sugar the rim of glasses before filling with tea or punch. Just run a small lemon wedge around the rim and place the glass upside down on a small plate of sugar. Tap off any extra sugar before filling.

Pineapple Limeade Cooler

*Kelly delCid
Troy, OH*

Just right for those patio parties...the kids love it too!

1 c. sugar
6 c. pineapple juice, chilled
1 c. lime juice

2 ltrs. sparkling water, chilled
Garnish: lime wedges

Shake sugar and juices together until sugar is dissolved; cover and refrigerate. Stir in sparkling water before serving over ice; garnish each glass with a lime wedge. Makes 16 servings.

Mint Ice Cubes

*Melody Taynor
Everett, WA*

*When served in iced tea, the tea becomes sweeter and mintier
as the cubes melt.*

6 c. water
1-1/2 c. sugar

1 t. lemon juice
48 mint leaves

Boil water, sugar and lemon juice together for 5 minutes; remove from heat and set aside to cool. Rub each mint leaf between your fingers to release its flavor; place one leaf in each of 48 ice cube compartments. Fill with sugar water; freeze. Makes 4 dozen.

Frozen grapes, strawberries and raspberries make flavorful ice cubes in frosty beverages. Freeze washed and dried fruit in a plastic zipping bag for up to 3 months...perfect for all the summer gatherings.

Basil-Mushroom Triangles

Mary Bettuchy
Duxbury, MA

Insert a toothpick into the top of each so guests can easily help themselves.

1/2 c. oil
6 fresh basil leaves

3 portabella mushrooms, sliced into wedges
salt and pepper to taste

Heat oil to sizzling in a small saucepan; add basil leaves. Turn off heat; set aside for 10 minutes. Strain oil into a 10" skillet, discarding basil leaves; reheat oil. Add mushroom pieces; sauté on both sides until golden, about 3 to 5 minutes. Remove from heat; sprinkle with salt and pepper. Serve warm. Serves 4 to 6.

Old dishes become tiered serving pieces when paired with a mug or candlestick. Center a mug on top of a dinner plate and top with a salad plate, gluing all if desired. Let dry, then serve up your favorite appetizers or desserts.

Appetizers 1~2~3

Snappy Asparagus Dip

Jane Gates
Saginaw, MI

Serve with crispy tortilla chips and fresh veggies.

1 lb. asparagus, trimmed,
  cooked and puréed
1 c. sour cream
1/2 c. salsa

1/8 t. lime juice
cayenne pepper, salt and pepper
  to taste

Combine all ingredients together; mix well. Cover and refrigerate until chilled. Makes about 2-1/2 cups.

Cheesy Potato Skins

Dolores Brock
Wellton, AZ

We love to dip these potato skins in ranch dressing.

4 potatoes, baked and halved
1/2 c. shredded Cheddar cheese
1/2 c. shredded mozzarella
  cheese

2 green onions, chopped
4 t. bacon bits

Place potatoes on a baking sheet; sprinkle with cheeses. Top with onions and bacon; heat under broiler until cheese melts. Serves 4.

If someone volunteers to pitch in with get-together preparations, or offers to bring a dish, let them! Just be sure to return the favor!

Baked Spinach Balls

Janet Pastrick
Fairfax, VA

To make ahead, just place spinach balls on baking sheets and freeze. Remove from freezer and place in heavy plastic zipping bags and return to freezer. When entertaining, remove from freezer, thaw on baking sheets and bake...so handy!

3 lbs. spinach, chopped, cooked
    and drained
2 c. herb-flavored stuffing mix
2 onions, minced
5 eggs, beaten
3/4 c. butter, melted

1/2 c. grated Parmesan cheese
2 cloves garlic, minced
1/2 t. salt
1 t. dried thyme
1/4 t. pepper

Combine all ingredients in a large mixing bowl; mix well. Shape into one-inch balls; arrange on ungreased baking sheets. Bake at 350 degrees for 15 minutes; serve warm. Makes 10 dozen.

When appetizers need to be served with a skewer, think beyond toothpicks...try sprigs of rosemary, bamboo picks or sugar cane spears.

Appetizers 1~2~3

Tortilla Roll-Ups

Kristin Freeman
Bixby, OK

Serve with salsa and guacamole for dipping.

8-oz. pkg. cream cheese,
   softened
1/3 c. salsa
1/4 c. green onion, chopped

1/2 t. garlic powder
1/2 t. chili powder
1/2 t. cumin
12-ct. pkg. flour tortillas

Blend cream cheese until light and fluffy; mix in salsa, onion, garlic powder, chili powder and cumin. Spread evenly over tortillas; roll up and refrigerate until firm, at least 2 hours. Cut into one-inch slices. Serves 12.

Carefree Cheese Spread

Bridget Dooley
Peru, IL

Whip up this tangy treat in no time. Serve with a loaf of French bread and crackers and guests can help themselves.

8-oz. pkg. cream cheese,
   softened
1 T. French salad dressing
1 T. chili sauce

3 to 4 drops Worcestershire
   sauce
garlic powder to taste

Blend all ingredients together until smooth. Makes one cup.

Laughter is brightest where food is best.
– Irish Proverb

Pizza by the Scoop

Tomi Russell
Algonquin, IL

Be sure to serve with sturdy crackers that can hold a lot!

15 to 20 pepperoni slices
2 c. shredded mozzarella cheese
2 c. shredded sharp Cheddar
  cheese

2 c. mayonnaise
1 sweet onion, chopped
4-1/2 oz. can diced green chiles

Arrange pepperoni slices on a paper towel and microwave for 20 to 30 seconds; pat with another paper towel and set aside. Combine cheeses, mayonnaise, onion and chiles in a mixing bowl; pour into a lightly greased 2-quart casserole dish. Layer pepperoni on top; cover and bake at 350 degrees for 45 minutes. Serves 8 to 10.

Please the whole gang by having an appetizer party! If your friends & family have different tastes, don't worry about deciding on the perfect main dish...just serve 4 to 5 different appetizers and everyone can choose their favorites.

Hearty Cheeseburger Bread

Marcy Venne
Russell, MA

Cut into one-inch slices for fun finger food.

2 lbs. ground beef, browned
1/2 t. garlic powder
1/4 c. butter

1 loaf French bread, cut in half
   horizontally
2 c. sour cream
3 c. shredded Cheddar cheese

Combine beef and garlic powder; set aside. Butter both halves of French bread; place on an ungreased baking sheet. Stir sour cream into beef mixture; spread onto bread. Sprinkle with cheese. Bake at 350 degrees for 15 to 20 minutes or until cheese melts; slice to serve. Serves 8 to 10.

Guests will love nibbling even more when appetizers are served on creative trays...try using a wooden cutting board, mirror, LP record, chessboard or an old-fashioned washboard. So fun!

Mini Manicotti

Emily Burns
Norwich, OH

A favorite Italian dish...in a new size!

1/2 lb. ground turkey, browned
1 clove garlic, minced
1 c. shredded mozzarella cheese
1/2 c. ricotta cheese
1/4 c. grated Parmesan cheese
1/2 t. dried Italian seasoning
1 t. lemon juice

1 egg, beaten
10-oz. pkg. frozen chopped
   spinach, thawed and drained
10 manicotti shells, cooked and
   rinsed
1-1/3 c. spaghetti sauce
2 T. shredded Parmesan cheese

Combine first 8 ingredients together in a large mixing bowl; stir in half
the spinach, reserving remaining for use in another recipe. Mix well;
spoon into shells. Slice each shell, diagonally, into 3 pieces; arrange in
an ungreased 13"x9" baking pan. Spoon spaghetti sauce on top; cover
with aluminum foil and bake at 350 degrees for 30 to 35 minutes.
Remove to a serving platter; sprinkle with Parmesan cheese.
Makes 30.

Quick and clever napkin rings! When serving pasta as an
appetizer or meal, use red & white checked napkins (or
just cut fabric into napkin-size squares) and slip each
through an uncooked manicotti shell.

Appetizers 1-2-3

Veggie-dillas

Glena Steele
Richfield, OH

An easy twist to a traditional quesadilla.

3/4 c. broccoli, chopped
1/4 c. carrots, shredded
1/4 c. green onion, sliced
2 T. water
6 6-inch flour tortillas

1 t. oil
2 c. shredded Cheddar cheese
Garnish: sour cream, salsa,
    sliced olives and sliced green
    onions

Combine broccoli, carrots, onions and water in a saucepan; heat until vegetables are crisp-tender. Drain; set aside. Brush one side of each tortilla with oil; place 3 tortillas oil-side down in an ungreased jelly-roll pan. Top with cheese; spread with vegetable mixture. Place remaining tortillas on top oil-side up; bake at 450 degrees until golden, about 6 minutes. Slice into wedges to serve; spoon desired garnishes on top. Serves 12.

Dress up a plain serving platter by arranging red and green cabbage leaves over the bottom of the plate...a lovely backdrop to the appetizer or main dish.

Easy Cheese Sticks

Margot Heinlein
Upper Arlington, OH

Melted cheese inside a crispy, golden shell.

1/3 lb. Monterey Jack cheese
1/3 lb. Cheddar cheese
1/3 lb. Swiss cheese
1/3 lb. mozzarella cheese
1 c. biscuit baking mix

1 t. paprika
1/2 c. milk
1 egg
oil for deep frying
marinara sauce

Cut cheeses into 3"x1/2" strips; place on a baking sheet. Wrap in plastic wrap; freeze for at least one hour. Blend baking mix, paprika, milk and egg together; set aside. Heat 2 inches oil in a deep stockpot to 375 degrees. Dip cheese strips in batter until coated; add to oil, heating until golden. Drain on paper towels; let stand 3 minutes before serving. Serve with marinara sauce on the side. Makes 2-1/2 dozen.

Ready-set-go snacks! When you need a little something extra for guests, but don't have any spare time, just pick up a few nibblers at the store. Assorted olives, fancy nuts, cream cheese and crackers, veggie sticks, cubed cheese and shrimp cocktail all make quick & easy treats.

Snappy Soups & Salads

Country Club Salad

Amy Jones
Buckhannon, WV

This salad recipe was shared with me by a good friend. A favorite recipe from their country club for parties and guests!

1-lb. pkg. bacon, crisply cooked
   and crumbled
1 head cauliflower, chopped

1 bunch romaine lettuce, torn
2 heads iceberg lettuce, torn
1 c. crumbled blue cheese

Toss all ingredients together in a large serving bowl; cover and refrigerate until chilled. Pour dressing on top before serving; refrigerating any excess dressing for later use. Toss gently. Serves 20.

Dressing:

1 c. cider vinegar
2 c. sugar
1 T. dry mustard

2 T. garlic powder
1/4 c. egg substitute
3 c. corn oil

Whisk all ingredients together.

When setting the table with stemmed glasses, open up colorful napkins, gather each in the middle and slip them, center down, into each glass...an instant dress-up for the table!

Snappy Soups & Salads

Wild Rice & Nut Soup

Linda Diepholz
Lakeville, MN

Toasted almonds add so much flavor to this special soup.

2 c. water
1/2 c. wild rice, uncooked
2 T. shallots, minced
2 T. butter
1/2 c. sliced mushrooms
1/4 c. all-purpose flour

4 c. chicken broth
1/4 c. carrots, grated
1/4 c. slivered almonds, toasted
1 c. half-and-half
Optional: 2 T. dry sherry
Garnish: fresh parsley, chopped

Bring water to a boil in a saucepan; add rice. Reduce heat; simmer, covered, for 45 minutes. Sauté shallots in butter in a 12" skillet until soft; add mushrooms and sauté for 2 additional minutes. Mix in flour; gradually stir in chicken broth until thickened. Add cooked rice, carrots and almonds; simmer for 5 minutes. Pour in half-and-half and sherry, if desired; heat through. Do not boil. Ladle into bowls; garnish with parsley. Serves 4.

It's a lovely thing; everyone sitting down together, sharing food.
- Alice May Brock

Oh-So-Quick Potato Soup

Flo Snodderly
North Vernon, IN

This recipe is perfect for just 2 but can easily be doubled or tripled!

1 cube chicken bouillon
1 c. water
1 c. mashed potatoes

1 T. butter
13-oz. can evaporated milk
  substitute

Combine all ingredients in a heavy saucepan; heat through without boiling, stirring until smooth. Makes 2 servings.

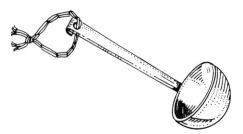

Traditional Clam Chowder

Amy Bachman
Waterville, PA

Bacon adds a smoky flavor to this rich dish.

2 c. red potatoes, peeled and
  cubed
1 c. onion, chopped
1/8 t. salt
1/8 t. pepper
2 c. water
4 6-1/2 oz. cans chopped
  clams, drained

4 c. milk
1 T. butter
8-oz. pkg. bacon, crisply cooked
  and crumbled
1 t. fresh parsley, chopped
2 T. all-purpose flour
3 cubes chicken bouillon

Place potatoes, onion, salt, pepper and water in a stockpot; boil until potatoes are tender, about 20 minutes. Add remaining ingredients; reduce heat. Simmer until thickened and heated through without boiling; stir often. Serves 4.

Snappy Soups & Salads

Broccoli-Cheese Soup

Donna Cloyd
Clinton, TN

If I'm in a hurry, I use onion flakes instead of chopping up an onion...quick and tearless!

1/4 c. margarine
1/2 c. onion, chopped
1/4 c. all-purpose flour
3 c. chicken broth
2 10-oz. pkgs. frozen chopped
   broccoli, thawed

4 cubes chicken bouillon
1/2 t. Worcestershire sauce
3 c. shredded Cheddar cheese
1-1/2 c. half-and-half
1 c. milk

Melt margarine in a 12" skillet; add onion and sauté until tender. Mix in flour; gradually add chicken broth, stirring until smooth. Add broccoli, bouillon and Worcestershire sauce; heat over medium heat until thickened and broccoli is tender, about 10 minutes. Mix in remaining ingredients; stir until cheese is melted, about 10 additional minutes. Makes 8 servings.

Get creative with placemats...try using mirror tiles, colorful sheets of scrapbook paper, road maps, bandannas, sheets of music or record album covers. Make them different every time!

Spiral Pasta Salad

Irene Senne
Aplington, IA

This colorful salad brightens the buffet table.

16-oz. pkg. tri-colored spiral
   pasta, cooked
2 carrots, shredded
1 sweet onion, chopped
1 green pepper, chopped
2 stalks celery, chopped
1 c. mayonnaise

1 c. vinegar
14-oz. can sweetened
   condensed milk
3/4 c. sugar
1 t. salt
1/4 t. pepper

Place pasta in a large serving bowl; fold in vegetables and set aside.
Combine remaining ingredients in a medium mixing bowl; blend well.
Pour over pasta; stir until well mixed. Cover and refrigerate overnight.
Serves 12 to 14.

Host friends in the garden this year. Greet everyone with
fresh iced tea served from a sparkling new watering can
and serve up salad using new garden trowels. So cute!

Snappy Soups & Salads

Picnic Spaghetti Salad

Ruth Cooksey
Plainfield, IN

After trying this recipe once, I knew it was perfect for taking to upcoming family reunions.

8-oz. pkg. spaghetti, coarsely
   broken
16-oz. pkg. coleslaw mix
1 onion, chopped

1 green pepper, chopped
1 c. mayonnaise
15-oz. jar coleslaw dressing

Prepare spaghetti according to package directions; drain and cool. Place in a large serving bowl; add remaining ingredients. Mix well; refrigerate until chilled. Serves 6 to 8.

Peanutty Crunch Salad

Carol Volz Begley
Beaver, PA

Wonderfully creamy and crunchy.

4 c. shredded cabbage
1 c. celery, chopped
1/2 c. sour cream
1/2 c. mayonnaise
1 t. salt
1/4 c. green onion, chopped

1/4 c. green pepper, chopped
1/2 c. cucumber, chopped
1 T. butter, softened
1/2 c. chopped peanuts
2 T. grated Parmesan cheese

Toss cabbage and celery together in a large serving bowl; cover and refrigerate until chilled. Whisk sour cream, mayonnaise, salt, onion, green pepper and cucumber together in a small mixing bowl; cover and refrigerate. Melt butter in a small skillet; sauté peanuts until golden. Right before serving, pour sour cream mixture over cabbage mixture; toss to coat. Sprinkle with peanuts and Parmesan cheese. Serves 6 to 8.

Black Bean Chili

Sharon Velenosi
Garden Grove, CA

This is my husband's favorite...and I never mind making it because it's so easy!

1 t. oil
2 onions, chopped
2 cloves garlic, minced
4-oz. can diced green chiles
2 t. chili powder
1 t. cumin

1 t. dried oregano
14-1/2 oz. can chopped
   tomatoes
2 15-oz. cans black beans,
   drained

Heat oil in a skillet; add onions and garlic. Sauté until soft; add remaining ingredients except for black beans. Mix well; bring to a boil over medium heat. Reduce heat; simmer for 10 minutes. Stir in beans; heat through. Serves 4 to 6.

3-Meat Slow-Cooker Chili

Beth Goblirsch
Minneapolis, MN

Spoon over a bed of rice or handful of taco chips...it feeds a crowd!

1 lb. ground beef, browned
1 lb. ground sausage, browned
1 lb. bacon, crisply cooked and
   crumbled

4 15-oz. cans tomato sauce
3 15-1/2 oz. cans kidney beans
chili seasoning to taste
15-1/4 oz. can corn, drained

Place first 3 ingredients in a greased slow cooker; stir in tomato sauce, kidney beans and chili seasoning. Heat on low setting for 4 to 6 hours; add corn during last hour of heating. Serves 8.

Snappy Soups & Salads

Cheeseburger Soup

Rhonda Gramstad
Brandon, SD

Serve with a juicy dill pickle on the side!

3/4 c. onion, chopped
3/4 c. carrots, shredded
1/2 c. celery, diced
1 t. dried basil
1/4 t. dried parsley
1/4 c. butter, divided
3 c. chicken broth
4 c. potatoes, peeled and diced

1/2 lb. ground beef, browned
1/4 c. all-purpose flour
8-oz. pkg. American cheese,
  cubed
1-1/2 c. milk
1/2 t. salt
1/4 t. pepper
1/2 c. sour cream

Sauté onion, carrots, celery, basil and parsley in one tablespoon butter in a 3-quart saucepan until tender, about 10 minutes; stir in broth, potatoes and ground beef. Bring to a boil; reduce heat and simmer, covered, for 10 minutes. Melt remaining butter in a small skillet; add flour, stirring until smooth and bubbly. Pour into soup; bring to a boil, stirring for 2 minutes. Reduce heat to low; stir in cheese, milk, salt and pepper. Continue stirring until cheese melts; remove from heat. Blend in sour cream before serving; serve warm. Serves 4 to 6.

It's the unexpected touches that make the biggest impressions. When serving soup or chili, offer guests a variety of fun toppings...fill bowls with shredded cheese, oyster crackers, chopped onions, sour cream and crunchy croutons then invite everyone to dig in!

Fabulous Feta Salad

Jen Sell
Farmington, MN

Make this salad into a main dish by topping with cooked chicken.

5-oz. pkg. spring-blend salad
   mix, divided
1/2 c. chopped pecans, toasted
3/4 c. crumbled feta cheese
6 slices bacon, crisply cooked
   and crumbled

11-oz. can mandarin oranges,
   drained and halved
grated Parmesan cheese to taste

Divide salad mix equally onto 4 serving plates; top each with equal servings pecans, feta, bacon and mandarin oranges. Sprinkle with Parmesan cheese; drizzle with poppy seed dressing. Serve immediately. Serves 4.

Poppy Seed Dressing:

1/2 c. mayonnaise
1/3 c. sugar
2 T. cider vinegar

1/4 c. milk
1 T. poppy seed

Mix mayonnaise and sugar together; whisk in remaining ingredients.

82

Snappy Soups & Salads

Asian Chicken Salad

Tammy Rowe
Bellevue, OH

A wonderful combination of ingredients you probably already have on hand.

2 boneless, skinless chicken breasts, cooked and shredded
1 bunch green onions, thinly sliced
1 head lettuce, shredded
2 T. poppy seed
2-oz. pkg. slivered almonds
3-oz. pkg. chow mein noodles

Toss the first 5 ingredients together in a serving bowl; right before serving, sprinkle with chow mein noodles and pour dressing on top. Serves 4.

Dressing:

1/4 c. vinegar
1/2 c. oil
2 T. flavor enhancer
1/2 t. salt
1/2 t. pepper

Whisk all ingredients together.

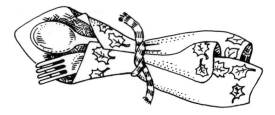

Balsamic vinegar really adds a zip to fresh salads. Pour some into a new spray bottle and set out for guests to use on their greens...spraying helps it go on easy without pouring too much!

Plaza Steak Soup

Jan Vaughn
Houston, TX

*My mom would buy this soup "to go" so much at the Plaza III
restaurant in Kansas City that the chef gave her the recipe.*

1/2 c. butter, melted
1 c. all-purpose flour
2 qts. water
2 c. steak, cooked and cut into
   bite-size pieces
1 c. celery, chopped
1 c. onion, chopped

1 c. carrots, chopped
2 c. frozen mixed vegetables
28-oz. can stewed tomatoes
1 T. flavor enhancer
2 T. beef bouillon granules
1 t. pepper

Whisk butter and flour together until smooth in a large stockpot; stir in
water and steak. Add remaining ingredients; bring to a boil. Reduce
heat; simmer for 3 to 4 hours. Serves 6.

Stack up each guest's place setting, then tie it up
with homespun and tuck fresh blossoms in the
knot...everyone will feel like they're sitting down with
their own special gift!

Snappy Soups & Salads

Pepper Pot Soup

Weda Mosellie
Phillipsburg, NJ

Especially great on chilly evenings with a crisp loaf of bread and a fresh salad.

1 lb. ground beef
1 onion, chopped
10-oz. pkg. sliced mushrooms
16-oz. pkg. bowtie pasta,
　uncooked

5 c. chicken broth
1 T. fresh parsley, chopped
1 T. pepper

Brown ground beef with onion and mushrooms; drain and set aside. Boil bowtie pasta for 5 minutes; drain and set aside. Pour chicken broth into a 5-quart Dutch oven; add all the ingredients. Bring to a boil; reduce heat and simmer, covered, for 20 minutes. Serves 8.

Winter Ranch Dumplings

Fawn McKenzie
Wenatchee, WA

Drop these into a favorite soup recipe as a hearty addition to dinner.

4 eggs
1-1/2 c. milk
1-1/2 t. salt

1-1/2 t. baking powder
2 to 4 c. all-purpose flour
chopped parsley to taste

Combine ingredients together in the order listed; drop into a boiling soup recipe by tablespoonfuls. Cover and reduce heat; simmer for 15 minutes without removing cover. Serves 4.

The company makes the feast.
- English Proverb

Pineapple-Pretzel Fluff

Julie Giffen
Xenia, OH

My famous contribution to carry-ins.

1 c. pretzels, crushed
1/2 c. butter, melted
1 c. sugar, divided
8-oz. pkg. cream cheese,
   softened

20-oz. can crushed pineapple,
   drained
12-oz. container frozen whipped
   topping, thawed

Combine crushed pretzels, butter and 1/2 cup sugar; press into the
bottom of an ungreased 13"x9" baking pan. Bake at 400 degrees for
7 to 9 minutes; set aside to cool. Break cooled mixture into coarse
pieces; set aside. Blend cream cheese and remaining sugar together in
a large mixing bowl until fluffy; fold in pineapple and whipped
topping. Sprinkle with pretzel mixture; toss gently. Serve immediately.
Serves 4.

Keep 'em cold! Fill a large galvanized tub with ice, then
nestle 2 to 3 serving bowls of salads or other cold sides
to keep chilled. Everyone can help themselves!

Snappy Soups & Salads

7-Fruit Salad

Laurie Parks
Westerville, OH

This salad is always a hit at summer get-togethers...and no one believes how easy it is!

1/2 c. lime juice
1/2 c. water
1/2 c. sugar
2 nectarines, peeled and thinly
   sliced
1 banana, thinly sliced
1 pt. blueberries

1 pt. strawberries, hulled and
   sliced
1-1/2 c. watermelon, scooped
   into balls
1-1/2 c. green grapes
1 kiwi, peeled and chopped

Whisk lime juice, water and sugar together in a medium mixing bowl until sugar dissolves; add nectarines and bananas, stirring to coat. Combine remaining ingredients in a 2-1/2 quart glass serving bowl; add nectarine mixture. Gently toss to mix; cover and refrigerate for one hour. Makes 8 to 10 servings.

Turn a strawberry pot into a garden-fresh centerpiece.
Place florist's foam in the center, then tuck
flowers in the openings that allow vines
to trail and arrange blooms on top.

Homemade Ham Salad

Marion Frisvold
Bloomington, MN

Try it with tuna or chicken instead of ham.

8-oz. pkg. spiral pasta, cooked
10-oz. pkg. frozen peas, cooked
2 lbs. cooked ham, diced
4 c. celery, thinly sliced
1-qt. jar mayonnaise-type salad
    dressing
3 t. salt

1 onion, minced
12 hard-boiled eggs, peeled and
    diced
2 4-oz. jars pimentos, drained
4-oz. pkg. chopped cashews
2 t. mustard
3 t. cider vinegar

Place all ingredients in a large serving bowl; mix well. Cover and refrigerate until chilled through. Serves 20.

Everyone loves a picnic and you don't need to head to the park to have one. Even if you don't have a deck or a patio, colorful blankets spread on the lawn (or in the living room!) create excitement for guests.

Snappy Soups & Salads

Light & Fruity Turkey Salad

Pat Habiger
Spearville, KS

A great way to use leftover turkey!

2-1/2 lbs. cooked turkey, diced
20-oz. can sliced water
  chestnuts, drained
2 lbs. seedless grapes, halved

2 c. celery, thinly sliced
20-oz. can pineapple chunks,
  drained
1-1/2 c. sliced almonds, toasted

Combine all ingredients together; mix well. Stir in dressing; cover and refrigerate overnight. Serves 8.

Dressing:

3 c. mayonnaise
1/2 T. curry powder

2 T. soy sauce
2 T. lemon juice

Whisk ingredients together.

A beachside centerpiece! Layer colored sand inside a clear glass vase or jar (use colors that match the tabletop) then tuck a taper candle inside.

Fix-Today, Better-Tomorrow Stew

Connie Carmack
Ballwin, MO

Serve with sourdough bread and sliced cheese...enjoy!

2 lbs. stew beef, cubed
2 14-1/2 oz. cans beef broth
2 10-3/4 oz. cans cream of
   mushroom soup
5 to 6 russet potatoes, cubed

1 c. baby carrots, halved
3 to 4 stalks celery, sliced
15-oz. can green beans, drained
2 onions, quartered

Place all ingredients in a Dutch oven; cover with aluminum foil. Bake at 325 degrees for 3-1/2 hours. Serves 4 to 6.

Thinking of a menu for guests? Let the season be your guide! Soups and stews chock full of harvest's bounty are just right for fall get-togethers, and juicy fruit salads are delightful in the summer. Not only will you get the freshest ingredients when you plan by the season, you'll get the best prices at the supermarket!

Snappy Soups & Salads

Hearty Vegetable-Beef Soup

Jennifer Rogers
Spotted Horse, WY

This good-for-you soup was handed down from my grandma. For family vacations we visited her in Ohio for two weeks and this soup was on the menu at least three times a week. I still make it in her old stockpot, always adding lots of love to each batch.

3 to 4-lb. bone-in chuck roast
1/2 onion, diced
3 potatoes, peeled and cubed
3 carrots, sliced
2 stalks celery, thinly sliced
15-oz. can cut green beans, drained
15-oz. can yellow wax beans, drained

15-oz. can butter or lima beans, drained
15-oz. can corn, drained
15-oz. can peas, drained
1/2 head cabbage, shredded
2 32-oz. cans cocktail vegetable juice

Place roast and onions in an 8-quart or larger stockpot; fill with enough water to just cover roast. Simmer until meat falls off bone, about one hour, adding additional water if necessary; set meat aside. Add potatoes, carrots, celery, beans, corn and peas to liquid in stockpot; bring to a boil. Stir in meat and reduce heat. Simmer until potatoes and carrots are tender, about 40 minutes; add cabbage and cocktail vegetable juice. Heat for 10 additional minutes; stir often. Serve warm. Serves 6 to 8.

Be sure to have plastic containers on hand to send everyone home with leftovers...if there are any!

Pumpkin Chowder

Sandy Westendorp
Grand Rapids, MI

This blend of everyday ingredients is anything but ordinary.

8-oz. pkg. bacon, diced
2 c. onions, chopped
2 t. curry powder
2 T. all-purpose flour
1-lb. pie pumpkin, peeled,
   seeded and chopped

2 potatoes, peeled and cubed
4 c. chicken broth
1 c. half-and-half
salt and pepper to taste
Garnish: toasted pumpkin seeds
   and sliced green onions

Brown bacon in a stockpot for 5 minutes; add onions. Sauté for
10 minutes; add curry and flour, stirring until smooth and creamy,
about 5 minutes. Add pumpkin, potatoes and broth; simmer until
potatoes are tender, about 15 minutes. Pour in half-and-half; season
with salt and pepper. Simmer for 5 minutes; do not boil. Spoon into
serving bowls; garnish with pumpkin seeds and onions. Serves 6.

Guests will love the smell of spicy pumpkin, and it's so
easy to create. Cut off the top of a pumpkin, scrape out
the insides and punch several holes in the pumpkin shell
with an apple corer. Rub cinnamon into the "walls"
of the pumpkin and place a tea light inside.

Snappy Soups & Salads

Veggie-Cheddar Chowder

Robin Outtrim
Camden, NY

Chock-full of goodness!

2 c. water
2 c. potatoes, diced
1/2 c. carrots, diced
1/2 c. celery, diced
1/4 c. onion, diced
1 t. salt

1/4 t. pepper
1/4 c. butter
1/4 c. all-purpose flour
2 c. milk
2 c. shredded Cheddar cheese
1 c. cooked ham, diced

Combine the first 7 ingredients in a large stockpot; bring to a boil. Boil until vegetables are tender, about 10 to 12 minutes. In the meantime, melt butter in a skillet; stir in flour until smooth. Gradually add milk, stirring until thickened; mix in cheese, stirring until melted. Pour into undrained vegetable mixture; add ham. Heat until warmed through, stirring constantly; do not boil. Serves 4.

There's nothing more cozy than a bowl of warm soup. For extra comfort, warm up oven-safe bowls in a 200-degree oven before filling...the soup (and guests) will stay warmer longer!

Family-Pleasing Coleslaw

Char Nix
Tustin, MI

For years I looked for a coleslaw recipe my family really liked...this one is a winner!

8 c. shredded cabbage
1/4 c. carrot, shredded
1/3 c. sugar
1/2 t. salt
1/8 t. pepper

1/4 c. milk
1/2 c. mayonnaise
1/4 c. buttermilk
1-1/2 T. white vinegar
2-1/2 T. lemon juice

Combine cabbage and carrots in a large serving bowl; gently mix. Set aside. Whisk remaining ingredients together; pour over cabbage mixture. Cover and refrigerate until chilled, about 4 hours; toss before serving. Serves 8 to 10.

Turn flower pot saucers into a set of colorful coasters. Use several shades of acrylic paint to brighten up the insides, let them dry and add to the tabletop or make stacks to give away as gifts.

Snappy Soups & Salads

Creamy Potato Salad

Francie Stutzman
Dalton, OH

A traditional classic with a twist.

2/3 c. Italian salad dressing
14 potatoes, baked, peeled and
   cubed
1-1/2 c. celery, chopped
2/3 c. green onions, sliced
8 hard-boiled eggs, peeled and
   separated

2 c. mayonnaise
1 c. sour cream
2-1/2 t. horseradish mustard
salt, pepper and celery seed to
   taste

Pour dressing over potatoes in a large mixing bowl; add celery and onions, tossing gently. Set aside. Chop egg whites; mix into potato mixture. Mash egg yolks in a medium mixing bowl; stir in mayonnaise, sour cream and mustard. Add to potato mixture; stir to coat. Season with salt, pepper and celery seed; cover and refrigerate until chilled, at least 4 hours. Serves 8 to 10.

Serve up slaw, salads and sides in colorful plastic or paper cups...clean up's a snap!

Slow-Cooker Chicken Chili

Erin Williams
Bayview, WI

This white chili really packs a punch!

1 lb. boneless, skinless chicken
    breasts, cubed
1 c. dried Great Northern beans,
    rinsed
1 clove garlic, minced
1 onion, chopped
2 t. dried oregano

1/2 t. salt
10-3/4 oz. can cream of chicken
    soup
5 c. water
1 t. cumin
4-oz. can diced green chiles
hot pepper sauce to taste

Combine all ingredients except cumin, chiles and hot pepper sauce in a 4-quart slow cooker; mix well. Heat on low setting for 8 to 10 hours or until juices run clear when chicken is pierced with a fork. Stir in remaining ingredients; heat through. Serves 8.

Don't have a table big enough for guests? No worries!
Just make sure food you serve can be held in
one hand and eaten with a spoon or fork...chili, soups,
sandwiches, followed by brownies or
cookies are great!

Snappy Soups & Salads

Dutch Oven Stew

Jennifer Sens
Mason, OH

This recipe has been in our family for at least 100 years! When the cool days of Fall roll around, everyone looks forward to this stick-to-your-ribs stew served over a bed of warm egg noodles.

1 c. all-purpose flour
1 t. paprika
1-lb. pkg. stew beef, cubed
1 to 2 T. oil
20-oz. bottle catsup

6-1/2 c. water
1 onion, chopped
2 T. sugar
2 T. vinegar
2 T. pickling spices

Combine flour and paprika in a shallow bowl; add beef, tossing to coat. Place beef in a Dutch oven; brown in oil. Add catsup, water, onion, sugar and vinegar; bring to a boil. Tie pickling spices in a square of muslin; add to beef mixture. Reduce heat; simmer for 3 hours, stirring occasionally. Remove spice bundle before serving. Serves 4.

Planning a Fathers' Day Feast or celebrating a new job? Slip button-down shirts over the backs of chairs, knot a tie around the collar and slip placecards in the pockets. So fun!

Extra-Easy Taco Salad

Linda Day
Wall, NJ

I sometimes like to add sliced black olives too...toss in
your favorite taco toppers!

1 head lettuce, shredded
2 tomatoes, diced
1 onion, diced
1 green pepper, diced
3/4 lb. ground beef, browned
   and cooled

2 c. shredded Cheddar cheese
2 8-oz. bottles Catalina salad
   dressing
8-oz. pkg. nacho-flavored
   tortilla chips, coarsely
   broken

Mix all ingredients together in a large serving bowl. Serve
immediately. Makes 6 to 8 servings.

A large glass bowl is a must-have for entertaining.
Whether it's used as a salad bowl, pasta dish or
filled with water and floating candles, it
works beautifully!

Snappy Soups & Salads

Marinated Tomatoes

Mary Baker
Fountain, NC

Absolutely delicious with tomatoes freshly picked from the garden.

1 clove garlic, minced
1/2 t. dried thyme
1/4 c. green onion, chopped
1/4 c. fresh parsley, minced
1 t. salt

1/4 t. pepper
6 tomatoes, thickly sliced
1/4 t. vinegar
1/3 c. oil

Combine garlic, thyme, onion, parsley, salt and pepper; sprinkle over tomatoes. Set aside. Mix vinegar and oil; pour over tomatoes. Cover; refrigerate for at least 2 hours. Mix gently before serving. Serves 10.

Dressed-Up Cucumbers

Holly Sutton
Middleburgh, NY

This country-fresh recipe goes great with grilled entrées.

1 c. mayonnaise
1/4 c. sugar
1/4 c. vinegar

1/4 t. salt
4 c. cucumbers, sliced

Combine the first 4 ingredients; mix well. Fold in cucumbers; cover and refrigerate for at least 2 hours. Serves 6 to 8.

All cooks, like all great artists, must have
an audience worth cooking for.
– Andre Simon

Thumbs-Up Cornbread Salad

Jana Timmons
Hendersonville, TN

Be sure to get your share early...it'll be gone before you know it!

8-1/2 oz. pkg. cornbread mix
24-oz. can pinto beans, drained
2 15-oz. cans corn, drained
1/4 c. sweet onion, diced
1 c. cherry tomatoes, quartered
1/2 c. bacon bits, divided

2 c. shredded 4-cheese blend
    cheese, divided
1/3 c. celery, chopped
1 c. sour cream
2 c. ranch salad dressing

Prepare cornbread according to package directions; set aside to cool. Crumble cornbread into a large serving bowl; add beans, corn, onion, tomatoes, 1/4 cup bacon bits, 1-1/2 cups cheese and celery. Toss well; set aside. In another bowl, mix sour cream and ranch dressing together; pour over cornbread mixture. Sprinkle with remaining bacon bits and cheese. Serves 10.

Try to arrange your grocery list according to the aisles in the supermarket...this will really cut down on time in the store running back & forth.

Snappy Soups & Salads

Bean & Ham Soup

Shannon Cronin
Hinton, IA

Comfort food!

1-lb. pkg. dried Great Northern
   beans, rinsed
8 c. water
1-1/2 lb. ham bone
2 potatoes, peeled and cubed
2 carrots, chopped
2 stalks celery, chopped
1 onion, chopped
3/4 t. dried thyme
1/2 t. salt
1/4 t. pepper
hot pepper sauce to taste

Combine beans and water in a large Dutch oven; bring to a boil. Reduce heat; simmer for 2 minutes. Remove from heat; cover and let stand for one hour. Bring beans to a boil again; add ham bone. Reduce heat; simmer for one hour. Remove ham bone; cool and remove meat from bone. Add meat to soup, discarding bone; stir in remaining ingredients. Cover; simmer until vegetables are tender, about 30 minutes. Serves 4 to 6.

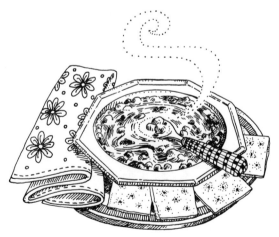

Getting the gang together for game day is fun and easy.
Celebrate with World Series Barbecue, Hoop Soups, or
Super Bowl Subs...they'll love it!

Cool Melon Salad

Jacqueline Kurtz
Reading, PA

There are so many pretty gelatin molds to use with this recipe.

3-oz. pkg. lime gelatin mix
2 c. warm water
1-1/2 c. cantaloupe, scooped
    into 1/2-inch balls

lettuce leaves
Optional: mayonnaise

Dissolve gelatin mix in warm water; pour into a lightly greased 4-cup mold. Fold in cantaloupe; refrigerate until firm. Unmold onto a serving platter lined with lettuce leaves; spread with mayonnaise, if desired. Makes 6 servings.

Make clever candleholders from melons to decorate for an afternoon gathering. Slice the top off of a cantaloupe, scoop out the insides and use cookie cutters to trace and cut designs on the outside. Set a tea light candle inside and enjoy!

Snappy Soups & Salads

Colorful Apple Salad

Jennifer Rudolph
Oakley, CA

Spoon this salad into a glass serving dish...it's so pretty!

6 Granny Smith apples, cored
  and chopped
6 Red Delicious apples, cored
  and chopped
3 stalks celery, diced

1/2 to 3/4 c. raisins
1 t. cinnamon
16-oz. container frozen whipped
  topping, thawed

Place apples in a large serving bowl; gently toss. Add remaining ingredients; stir gently. Serve immediately. Serves 12.

Frozen Cranberry Salad

Sue Dunlap
Huntsville, AL

Spoon into muffin cups and freeze for individual servings.

2 3-oz. pkgs. cream cheese,
  softened
2 T. mayonnaise
2 T. sugar
8-oz. can crushed pineapple

16-oz. can whole cranberry
  sauce
1/2 c. chopped pecans
1 c. frozen whipped topping,
  thawed

Blend cream cheese until light; mix in mayonnaise, sugar and pineapple. Fold in cranberry sauce and pecans; stir in whipped topping. Spread into an ungreased 11"x8" freezer-safe pan; cover with plastic wrap. Freeze; thaw slightly before serving. Cut into squares to serve. Makes 24 servings.

Fruity Marshmallow Salad

Kim Ripley
Elmira, NY

My family enjoys this salad at every holiday...and sometimes in between!

20-oz. can pineapple chunks,
  drained
14-1/2 oz. jar maraschino
  cherries, drained and halved
11-oz. can mandarin oranges,
  drained
1/2 lb. grapes, halved
10-1/2 oz. pkg. mini
  marshmallows

2 bananas, sliced
1 c. frozen orange juice
  concentrate, thawed
1/2 c. chopped walnuts
1-1/2 pts. whipping cream
1/4 c. sugar
1 t. vanilla extract

Combine pineapple, cherries, oranges, grapes and marshmallows;
refrigerate overnight. Soak bananas in orange juice for 30 minutes;
stir in walnuts. Set aside. Whip cream with sugar and vanilla, blending
until stiff peaks form; spoon into a large serving bowl. Fold in fruit
mixtures; stir gently. Serves 8.

Having girlfriends over for dinner? Tie different colors of
satin bows to stemmed glasses before
filling with bubbly. Easy and elegant
beverage charms...cheers!

Simply Delicious Sides & Breads

Fabulous Baked Potato Casserole

Ginia Johnston
Greeneville, TN

This is my most requested recipe...it always goes first at every gathering.

6 to 7 potatoes, peeled and
    cubed
2 c. shredded Cheddar cheese
1 c. mayonnaise

1/2 c. sour cream
1 onion, diced
6 slices bacon, crisply cooked
    and crumbled

Place potatoes in a large saucepan; barely cover with water. Boil until fork tender, about 20 minutes; drain and set aside to cool. Combine cheese, mayonnaise, sour cream and onion together; mix in potatoes, tossing gently to coat. Spread potato mixture in a buttered 13"x9" baking pan; sprinkle bacon on top. Bake at 350 degrees until golden and bubbly, about 20 to 25 minutes. Serves 8.

What a welcome! Prop up a blackboard by the front door and use chalk to print the menu...guests will feel like they're dining in a charming bistro!

Simply Delicious Sides & Breads

All-Time Favorite Corn Casserole

Jackie Balla
Walbridge, OH

So good and easily doubled if expecting extras around the table.

2 15-oz. cans shoepeg corn,
   drained
10-3/4 oz. can cream of celery
   soup
1/2 c. onion, chopped

1 c. shredded Cheddar cheese
1/2 c. sour cream
1/2 c. butter, melted
1 sleeve round buttery crackers,
   crushed

Combine the first 5 ingredients in a buttered 2-quart casserole dish;
set aside. Mix butter and crushed crackers together; sprinkle over
corn mixture. Bake at 350 degrees for 45 minutes. Serves 4 to 6.

Green Beans in Garlic Butter

Carmen Turner
Key West, FL

Select the most slender green beans for the freshest taste.

1 c. chicken broth
salt and pepper to taste
2 lbs. green beans, trimmed and
   halved

4 cloves garlic, thinly sliced
1/4 c. butter, melted

Add chicken broth, salt and pepper to a stockpot; bring to a boil. Add
green beans; heat until tender, stirring often. Drain; place in a serving
bowl. Sauté garlic in butter in a small skillet until golden; pour over
green beans, tossing gently to coat. Serve warm. Makes 6 servings.

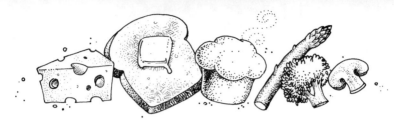

Tomato-Zucchini Casserole

Jeanne Hodack
Norwich, NY

This recipe has always been a hit at our church picnics. My family enjoys this as a main dish along with crusty bread and fresh fruit.

1 c. shredded Cheddar cheese
1/3 c. grated Parmesan cheese
1/2 t. dried oregano
1/2 t. dried basil
1 clove garlic, minced
3 zucchini, thinly sliced and divided

2 tomatoes, sliced and divided
1/4 c. butter
2 T. onion, minced
1/2 c. Italian-seasoned bread crumbs

Combine cheeses, oregano, basil and garlic; set aside. Spread half the zucchini and half the tomatoes in a greased 8"x8" baking pan; sprinkle with half the cheese mixture. Repeat layers; set aside. Melt butter in a small skillet; add onion and sauté until transparent. Remove from heat; stir in bread crumbs. Sprinkle over cheese layer; cover with aluminum foil. Bake at 350 degrees for 30 minutes; uncover and bake for an additional 25 minutes. Serves 8.

Find a great chandelier at a flea market? Add some new taper candles and set it in the center of the table for a quick centerpiece...no need for hanging!

Simply Delicious Sides & Breads

Broccoli-Cauliflower Bake
Jo Ann

Frozen veggies make this dish a cinch.

16-oz. pkg. frozen broccoli cuts
16-oz. pkg. frozen cauliflower
  flowerets
1 c. onion, chopped
4 T. butter, divided
2 T. all-purpose flour
1 t. salt
1/2 t. garlic powder

1/2 t. dried basil
1/4 t. pepper
1-1/4 c. milk
2 3-oz. pkgs. cream cheese with
  chives, cubed
3/4 c. bread crumbs
3 T. grated Parmesan cheese

Prepare broccoli and cauliflower according to package directions; drain.
Place in a large saucepan; set aside. Sauté onion in 2 tablespoons
butter until tender; stir in flour, salt, garlic powder, basil and pepper.
Add milk; heat and stir until bubbly and thickened. Mix in cream
cheese; stir until melted. Pour over vegetables; stir to mix. Spread in
an ungreased 2-quart casserole dish; set aside. Melt remaining butter;
add bread crumbs and Parmesan cheese, mix until crumbly. Sprinkle
over casserole; bake at 400 degrees for 25 to 30 minutes. Makes
12 servings.

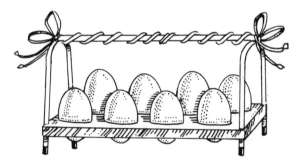

Quickly dress up a table by filling a glass bowl with
seasonal objects...pine cones and ornaments during
Winter, dyed eggs in Spring, seashells and sand in
Summer and shiny apples during Fall.

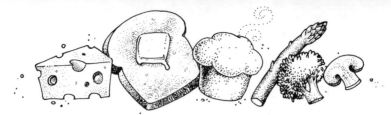

Parmesan & Basil Pull-Apart Bread
Judith Shipley
Camby, IN

Serve warm with extra butter or pizza sauce on the side for dipping.

25-oz. pkg. frozen roll dough
1 c. grated Parmesan cheese
1 T. dried basil

1 t. salt
1/2 c. butter, clarified

Thaw dough in the refrigerator overnight; slice each roll in half. Combine Parmesan cheese, basil and salt; set aside. Dip bread rounds in butter; roll in cheese mixture. Place in a greased Bundt® pan; let rise for 2-1/2 hours. Bake at 375 degrees for 20 to 25 minutes; invert on a serving plate. Makes 20 servings.

Tasty Garlic Bread
Renae Scheiderer
Beallsville, OH

A classic addition to spaghetti or lasagna.

1/3 c. butter
12 slices bread

1/2 t. garlic salt
3 T. grated Parmesan cheese

Spread butter equally on one side of each bread slice; cut each slice in half. Arrange butter-side up on an aluminum foil-lined baking sheet; sprinkle with garlic salt and Parmesan cheese. Broil 4 inches from the heat until lightly toasted, about one to 2 minutes. Makes 24 servings.

In cooking, as in all arts, simplicity is
the sign of perfection.
– Curnonsky

Herb Biscuits Supreme

La Verne Fang
Delavan, IL

You won't want to make biscuits any other way once you've tried these!

1-1/2 c. all-purpose flour	1 t. sugar
3 t. baking powder	1/2 t. dill weed
1/4 t. salt	1-1/2 t. dried chives
1/4 t. cream of tartar	1 c. whipping cream

Mix flour, baking powder, salt, cream of tartar and sugar together; stir in dill weed and chives. Mix well. Pour in cream; stir with a fork until just moistened. Place dough on a floured surface; knead. Roll out to a 3/4-inch thickness; cut into rounds with a biscuit cutter. Bake at 450 degrees on an ungreased baking sheet for 10 to 12 minutes. Makes 8.

Make a big impression with little effort. Cover the bottom of a salad plate with olive oil and drizzle a little balsamic vinegar on top...serve it alongside warm bread for dipping. Try filling saucers with oil and vinegar at each place setting for individual servings.

Asparagus-Onion Casserole

Joely Flegler
Edmond, OK

A tender and crunchy combination in one great dish.

1-lb. pkg. asparagus, trimmed
    and cut into one-inch pieces
2 onions, sliced
5 T. butter, divided
2 T. all-purpose flour
1 c. milk

3-oz. pkg. cream cheese, cubed
1 t. salt
1/8 t. pepper
1/2 c. shredded Cheddar cheese
1 c. bread crumbs

Sauté asparagus and onions in one tablespoon butter until crisp-tender, about 8 minutes; transfer to an ungreased 1-1/2 quart casserole dish. Set aside. Melt 2 tablespoons butter in a saucepan; whisk in flour until smooth. Gradually add milk; heat and stir until thickened, about 2 minutes. Reduce heat; mix in cream cheese, salt and pepper, stirring until cheese melts. Pour over asparagus and onions; sprinkle with Cheddar cheese. Melt remaining butter in a small skillet; remove from heat. Add bread crumbs; toss gently. Sprinkle over casserole; bake at 350 degrees for 35 to 40 minutes. Serves 4 to 6.

Dime-store treasures! Seek out vintage silver serving pieces...jazz them up by hot gluing beads, rhinestones, buttons or tiny silk flowers on the handles.

Crispy Wild Rice

Mary Jo Babiarz
Spring Grove, IL

Cheesy, crunchy and delicious!

2 6-oz. pkgs. long-grain and
   wild rice mix
8-oz. jar pasteurized processed
   cheese sauce
8-oz. can sliced water chestnuts,
   drained

6-oz. jar sliced mushrooms,
   drained
2-oz. jar diced pimentos,
   drained
2.8-oz. can French fried onions,
   crushed

Prepare rice mix according to package directions; place in a mixing bowl. Mix in cheese sauce, water chestnuts, mushrooms and pimentos; spread in a lightly buttered 11"x7" baking pan. Cover with aluminum foil; bake at 325 degrees for 20 minutes. Uncover; top with French fried onions. Bake 5 additional minutes. Serves 4 to 6.

Have a cupboard full of mismatched dishes and a drawer full of mismatched flatware? A combination of different colors and patterns makes fun settings for the table, so go ahead and mix it up!

Grandma's Biscuits

Kristie Rigo
Friedens, PA

*When Grandma bakes these, my 2 teenage boys
eat them all in one sitting!*

3 c. biscuit baking mix   2/3 c. milk
2 3-oz. pkgs. cream cheese

Place baking mix in a large mixing bowl; cut in cream cheese until crumbly. Add milk; mix until soft dough forms. Pat dough into a circle, 1/2-inch thick, on a surface lightly dusted with biscuit baking mix; cut into biscuits with a 2-inch biscuit cutter. Arrange on lightly greased baking sheets; bake at 450 degrees until golden, about 8 to 10 minutes. Makes one dozen.

Try different toppers for Grandma's Biscuits. Before baking, brush tops with melted butter then sprinkle on treats like chocolate chips, cinnamon and sugar, chopped nuts, shredded cheese or diced pepperoni.

Simply Delicious Sides & Breads

Kitchen's Best Dinner Rolls

Marilyn Kent
Clontarf, MN

There's nothing quite like the smell of homemade bread.

4-1/2 to 5 c. all-purpose flour,
   divided
1/4 c. sugar
1 pkg. active dry yeast

1 t. salt
1 c. milk
1/2 c. water
1/4 c. margarine

Mix 1-1/2 cups flour, sugar, yeast and salt together in a large mixing bowl; set aside. Heat milk, water and margarine in a saucepan to 120 degrees as measured by a candy thermometer; blend into flour mixture. Add remaining flour, 1/2 cup at a time, until a soft dough forms; knead 2 to 3 minutes. Shape into 12 rolls; arrange in a greased 13"x9" baking pan. Set aside to rise until double in bulk; bake at 375 degrees for 20 to 25 minutes. Makes one dozen.

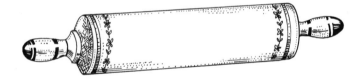

Make Kitchen's Best Dinner Rolls extra special. Just before baking, mix together 3 tablespoons flour, 3/4 teaspoon hot water and 3 tablespoons softened butter. Pipe mixture onto rolls in fun designs...flowers, snowflakes and smiley faces look great!

6-Bean Slow-Cooker Bake

Doreen DeRosa
New Castle, PA

Great for a crowd!

15-1/2 oz. can chickpeas
15-oz. can lima beans
15-1/2 oz. can hot chili beans
14-1/2 oz. can green beans
15-oz. can yellow wax beans
16-oz. can pork & beans
10-3/4 oz. can tomato soup
1-1/4 c. sugar

2 T. barbecue sauce
2 T. mustard
6-oz. can tomato paste
1 lb. bacon, crisply cooked and
  crumbled
1-lb. pkg. hot sausage, sliced
  and browned

Add all ingredients to a slow cooker; mix well. Heat on low setting
until warmed through, about 4 hours. Serves 10 to 12.

An instant hit! Core an apple, then scoop out
the insides, leaving at least 1/4-inch thick
sides...set each on a serving plate
and fill with baked beans.

Simply Delicious Sides & Breads

New England Baked Beans

Nelle Stinson-Smith
Mobile, AL

This All-American dish is a slow-poke in the oven, but it's definitely worth the wait!

8-oz. pkg. dried Great Northern
    beans
1/2 lb. bacon, diced
2 t. salt

2 T. brown sugar, packed
1/4 c. molasses
1/2 t. dry mustard
2 t. Worcestershire sauce

Soak beans in cold water overnight; drain. Place in a large Dutch oven; cover with water. Boil until skins break; drain. Pour into a buttered roasting pan; stir in bacon. Pour boiling water on top until just covered; set aside. Mix remaining ingredients together; add one cup boiling water. Stir into beans; cover. Bake at 250 to 300 degrees for 6 to 8 hours, adding additional water to keep beans covered. Uncover during last half hour to brown the bacon. Serves 6 to 8.

Microwave "Baked" Beans

Andrea Kahlenbeck
Columbus, IN

A 5-minute side dish!

16-oz. can pork & beans
1/2 c. brown sugar, packed
1 T. catsup

dried, minced onion
pepper to taste

Combine first 3 ingredients in a microwave-safe bowl; mix well. Sprinkle with enough dried onion to lightly cover the top; mix well. Add pepper to taste; cover and microwave on high until thickened, about 4 minutes. Stir after each minute. Serves 4.

Marvelous Mashed Potatoes

Janie Branstetter
Duncan, OK

Need a side dish in a hurry? This one couldn't be easier.

4 c. instant mashed potato
    flakes
8-oz. pkg. cream cheese, cubed
1 bunch green onions, chopped

2 T. fresh parsley, minced
1 T. butter
paprika to taste

Prepare mashed potatoes according to package directions, substituting cream cheese for butter; stir in onions and parsley. Spoon into a buttered one-quart casserole dish; dot with butter. Sprinkle with paprika; bake at 400 degrees for 30 minutes. Serves 6.

Easy Scalloped Potatoes

Dawn Miller
Mount Morris, MI

Cut down on prep time by leaving the peel on the potatoes...just as tasty!

7 potatoes, peeled, sliced and
    divided
1 onion, chopped and divided
10-3/4 oz. can cream of
    mushroom soup, divided

1/2 c. cooked ham, cubed and
    divided
Optional: 2 c. shredded Cheddar
    cheese

Arrange a third of the potato slices in the bottom of a lightly buttered 2-quart casserole dish; add a third of the onion, a third of the soup and a third of the ham. Repeat layers twice; sprinkle cheese on top, if desired. Bake for 350 degrees for 45 to 55 minutes. Serves 4.

Simply Delicious Sides & Breads

Buttermilk Hushpuppies

Liz Plotnick-Snay
Gooseberry Patch

Perfect for a BBQ!

2 c. cornmeal
1 c. all-purpose flour
1 T. sugar
1 T. baking powder
1/2 t. baking soda
1-1/2 t. salt
1 t. pepper

1 egg
1 t. hot pepper sauce
1-1/2 c. buttermilk
1 c. onion, minced
1 c. corn
oil for deep frying

Combine the first 7 ingredients in a medium mixing bowl; set aside.
Whisk egg and hot pepper sauce together; stir in buttermilk. Add to
cornmeal mixture; stir until just moistened. Fold in onion and corn;
drop by tablespoonfuls into hot oil. Heat until golden, turning once;
drain on paper towels. Makes 3 dozen.

Group several pillar candles on a tray or in a shallow bowl
in the center of the table, then surround the bases with
twigs, rocks and leaves...now you have a campfire indoors.
Get out the s'mores!

Lemon-Rice Pilaf

Esther Robinson
Brownsville, TX

A complement to any main dish...garnish each serving with a lemon slice.

2 T. butter
1/2 c. long-grain rice, uncooked
1/2 c. vermicelli, uncooked and
   broken into 1-inch pieces

1-3/4 c. chicken broth
1 T. lemon zest
1 T. fresh parsley, chopped

Melt butter in a saucepan; add rice and vermicelli. Cook until golden; add broth. Bring to a boil; reduce heat. Cover; simmer for 15 to 20 minutes. Stir in lemon zest and parsley. Serves 4.

When garnishing with lemon slices, do it with a twist! Cut thin slices with a paring knife, then cut from center to rind. Hold edges and twist in opposite directions.

Simply Delicious Sides & Breads

Marinated Carrots

Gloria Robertson
Midland, TX

Fresh carrots and green peppers team up in this vegetable side dish.

2 lbs. carrots, sliced
1 green pepper, chopped
1 onion, chopped
1 c. tomato juice
1/8 t. salt
1/8 t. pepper

1/3 c. white vinegar
1 c. sugar
1 t. mustard
1 t. Worcestershire sauce
1/2 c. oil

Boil carrots until crisp-tender; rinse in ice water and drain. Add pepper and onion; set aside. Combine remaining ingredients in a saucepan; heat over low heat until warmed through, stirring often. Pour over carrot mixture; cover and refrigerate overnight. Serves 8 to 10.

Escalloped Apples

Alison O'Keeffe
Westerville, OH

Dress up your dinner with this sweet side.

10 c. tart apples, cored, peeled
  and sliced
1/3 c. sugar
2 T. cornstarch

1 t. cinnamon
1/4 t. nutmeg
2 T. chilled butter, sliced

Place apples in a 2-1/2 quart microwave-safe bowl; set aside. Combine sugar, cornstarch, cinnamon and nutmeg; sprinkle over apples. Toss gently to coat; dot with butter. Cover and microwave on high until apples are tender, about 15 minutes, stirring every 5 minutes. Makes 8 to 10 servings.

Savory Corn

Jo Anne Hayon
Sheboygan, WI

This is my daughter's favorite recipe!

10-oz. pkg. frozen corn,
   partially thawed
1/4 c. butter
1 t. cornstarch
1/2 t. sugar

1/4 t. salt
1/4 t. dried tarragon or
   dried basil
1/8 t. pepper

Combine all ingredients in an ungreased one-quart, microwave-safe bowl; cover and heat on high for 6 to 7 minutes, stirring twice during heating. Serves 4.

Awesome Onion Casserole

Deborah Lamoree
Mesa, AZ

Your guests will be amazed by the flavor of this dish...just don't tell them how easy it is to prepare!

2 yellow onions, sliced,
   separated into rings and
   divided
1 red onion, sliced, separated
   into rings and divided
12 green onions, chopped and
   divided

1 t. pepper, divided
6-oz. pkg. crumbled blue cheese
10-oz. pkg. Havarti cheese,
   grated
3 T. butter, sliced
3/4 c. dry white wine or chicken
   broth

Layer half the yellow, red and green onions in a lightly buttered 13"x9" baking pan; sprinkle with 1/2 teaspoon pepper. Add blue cheese; layer remaining onions on top. Sprinkle with remaining pepper; layer Havarti cheese on onions. Dot with butter; pour wine or broth over the top. Bake at 350 degrees for one hour or until onions are tender. Serves 6.

Oh-So-Creamy Hashbrowns

Sandy Watters
Altoona, PA

A wonderful potato dish without having to peel a single potato!

30-oz. pkg. frozen shredded
   hashbrowns, partially
   thawed
1 c. sour cream
1 c. butter, melted and divided

2 10-3/4 oz. cans cream of
   chicken soup
1 onion, diced
50 to 60 round buttery crackers,
   crushed

Mix hashbrowns, sour cream, 1/2 cup butter, soup and onion together; spread in a buttered 13"x9" baking pan. Set aside. Pour remaining butter over crushed crackers; toss gently. Sprinkle over potato mixture; bake at 350 degrees for one hour. Serves 8 to 10.

When shopping for cloth napkins, be sure to pick up an extra one...use it to wrap around a flower pot, pitcher or pail and you'll always have a matching centerpiece.

Homestyle Dressing

Therese Reid
Rhodesdale, MD

Moist and tasty!

1 onion, chopped
2 stalks celery, chopped
1/2 c. margarine
1/2 T. poultry seasoning
1-1/2 loaves bread, cubed
2 10-3/4 oz. cans cream of
   chicken soup

2 10-1/2 oz. cans chicken broth
4 eggs
1/4 t. dried sage
1/2 t. pepper
1 t. salt

Sauté onion and celery in margarine; set aside. Combine poultry seasoning with the bread; add remaining ingredients. Spread in a buttered roaster; cover and bake at 400 degrees for one hour. Serves 6 to 8.

There's nothing easier than sprucing up a table with flowers...cluster a small bunch of garden roses in a teapot, add a bouquet of daffodils to an old-fashioned milk bottle or arrange fresh daisies in a watering can. It's so simple!

Simply Delicious Sides & Breads

Herbed Onion Bread

Lorie McGuire
Erie, KS

Slice and serve with whipped butter.

1-1/2 c. onion, diced
2 T. butter
3 c. biscuit baking mix
1 egg

1 c. milk
1 t. dried basil
1 t. dill weed

Sauté onion in butter in a skillet until tender, about 5 to 7 minutes; remove from heat. Combine remaining ingredients in a large mixing bowl; stir in onion until just blended. Spoon into a greased 9"x5" loaf pan; bake at 350 degrees for 55 to 60 minutes. Cool; remove from pan. Makes 8 servings.

Clover Tea Rolls

Renae Scheiderer
Beallsville, OH

A classic you'll make again and again.

2 c. all-purpose flour
1/4 c. sugar
3/4 t. baking soda
1/2 t. salt

1/3 c. shortening
1/2 c. milk
3 T. lemon juice

Sift together flour, sugar, baking soda and salt in a large bowl. Cut in shortening until mixture resembles coarse crumbs. Combine milk and lemon juice; quickly stir into flour mixture to form a soft dough. Turn out onto a lightly floured surface; knead slightly. Form into small marble-size balls. Place 3 balls into each greased muffin cup; bake at 450 degrees for 15 minutes or until golden. Makes one dozen.

Garden Skillet

Vickie

Personalize with your favorite veggies...try broccoli, squash, tomatoes or carrots. Make it different every time!

2-1/2 c. bowtie pasta, uncooked
2 T. butter
1 t. minced garlic
2 zucchini, cut into 1/2-inch
   slices

1 red onion, sliced into thin
   wedges
1-1/2 T. fresh basil, chopped
8-oz. pkg. Cheddar cheese, diced
salt and pepper to taste

Prepare bowtie pasta according to package directions; drain and set aside. Melt butter in a 10" skillet; sauté garlic until golden. Add zucchini, red onion and basil; heat over medium heat until tender, about 4 to 6 minutes. Stir in pasta; heat through. Add cheese, salt and pepper; toss gently. Serve immediately. Serves 4 to 6.

Looking for a centerpiece to go with a garden-fresh meal? Slice a watermelon in half and use half as a vase...don't even bother to hollow it out! Simply tuck flower stems right in the melon, and the water inside will help keep them vibrant.

Simply Delicious Sides & Breads

Roasted Root Vegetables

Jennifer Wickes
Pine Beach, NJ

Roasting brings out the natural sweetness of vegetables.

4 red potatoes, quartered
4 turnips, quartered
2 parsnips, cut into one-inch
   slices
2 carrots, thickly sliced
1 yam, cut into one-inch slices

16 pearl onions, peeled
4 beets, quartered
8 cloves garlic
1/2 c. olive oil
2 T. fresh rosemary, chopped
salt and pepper to taste

Wash and rinse vegetables; spread on paper towels to drain, patting each piece dry. Place in a large plastic zipping bag; add remaining ingredients. Close bag; turn several times to coat vegetables evenly. Spread mixture in a roasting pan; bake at 450 degrees for one hour. Serves 8.

Be sure to place warm melted butter on the table for guests to brush over vegetables or rolls. Make a natural butter brush by bundling sprigs of fresh herbs such as thyme, oregano, parsley or rosemary, then bind them together with jute...adds extra flavor too!

Praline-Topped Butternut Squash

Nancy Kowalski
Southbury, CT

When we're invited to a family gathering I'm always asked to bring this dish.

2 butternut squash, peeled and cubed	2 eggs, beaten
7 T. margarine, divided	1/2 t. cinnamon
1/2 t. salt	1/2 c. brown sugar, packed
1/8 t. pepper	1/8 t. nutmeg
	1/2 c. chopped walnuts

Boil squash in water until soft; drain. Spoon into a blender; purée until smooth. Transfer to a saucepan; stir in 4 tablespoons margarine, salt and pepper. Warm through; remove from heat. Mix in eggs; spread into a greased one-quart casserole dish. Set aside. Combine cinnamon, brown sugar, remaining margarine, nutmeg and walnuts; sprinkle over squash mixture. Bake at 350 degrees for 30 minutes. Serves 8.

Oh-so clever! Invite friends over for a Fall gathering, and before they arrive, go outside to collect large, colorful leaves...place one under each glass at the table to use as coasters.

Pineapple-Topped Sweet Potatoes
Linda Littlejohn
Greensboro, NC

My family won't eat sweet potatoes any other way!

2 c. sweet potatoes, boiled and
    mashed
1/4 t. salt
1/4 c. margarine, softened

1 c. sugar
2 eggs
1/4 c. milk
1 t. vanilla extract

Combine all ingredients together; spoon into an ungreased 2-quart casserole dish. Spoon on topping; bake at 350 degrees for 30 minutes. Serves 8.

Pineapple Topping:

1/4 c. all-purpose flour
1/2 c. sugar
1 egg

1/4 c. margarine, softened
8-oz. can crushed pineapple,
    drained

Combine flour and sugar; stir in egg and margarine. Fold in pineapple; mix well.

Dance fresh fruits and veggies down the center of the table...decorating is done!

Impossible Garden Pie

Suellen Anderson
Rockford, IL

It's just not possible that this delicious side dish is so quick & easy to make!

2 c. zucchini, chopped
1 c. tomatoes, chopped
1/2 onion, chopped
1/3 c. grated Parmesan cheese
1/2 t. dill weed

1/2 c. biscuit baking mix
2 eggs
1 t. salt
1/4 t. pepper

Combine vegetables; spread in a greased 9" deep-dish pie pan. Set aside. Blend remaining ingredients together until smooth; pour over vegetables. Bake at 350 degrees for 50 to 55 minutes; cool for 5 minutes before serving. Serves 6 to 8.

Have a fun collection of pie birds? Use them for placecard holders! Just cut out cardstock, print on names, then nestle them right in the beaks. So cute!

Harvest Zucchini Pie

Jackie Smulski
Lyons, IL

This is a traditional fall favorite in my family.

8-oz. tube refrigerated crescent
  rolls
2 zucchini, sliced
1 clove garlic, minced
1 onion, chopped
2 T. olive oil
2 T. fresh parsley, minced

1/4 t. pepper
4-oz. can mushrooms, drained
4-oz. carton egg substitute
1/3 c. grated Parmesan cheese
1/2 c. shredded Monterey Jack
  cheese

Separate crescent dough into 8 triangles; line a greased 9" pie pan
with dough, facing points toward the center. Press seams together;
set aside. Sauté zucchini, garlic and onion in oil; add parsley and
pepper. Spoon into crust; add mushrooms and egg substitute. Sprinkle
with cheeses; bake at 375 degrees for 35 to 40 minutes. Let stand
5 minutes before serving. Makes 6 to 8 servings.

On a hot day, just before guests arrive, stand up bottles
of well-chilled soda and water in galvanized box
planters, then line arrange them down the center
of the table. Guests can help themselves
to refreshments throughout the meal!

Spinach Mashed Potatoes

Vicki Ault
Syracuse, OH

Skip the gravy with these mashed potatoes...they're so flavorful, they don't need any!

6 to 8 potatoes, peeled and
    boiled
1/2 c. margarine
3/4 c. sour cream
1 t. salt
1/4 t. pepper

1 t. sugar
2 T. onion, chopped
1 c. shredded Cheddar cheese,
    divided
10-oz. pkg. frozen chopped
    spinach, cooked and drained

Mash potatoes with margarine; stir in sour cream, salt, pepper, sugar, onion and 3/4 cup cheese. Fold in spinach; spoon into a greased 13"x9" baking pan. Sprinkle with remaining cheese; bake at 350 degrees for 25 to 30 minutes. Serves 6.

Rosemary Potatoes

Gayle Burns
Bloomington, IN

So simple, yet extraordinarily delicious.

4 to 6 red potatoes, peeled and
    quartered
1 to 2 t. dried rosemary, crushed
2 cloves garlic, minced

salt and pepper to taste
1/4 c. olive oil
2 T. lemon juice

Mix all ingredients together; spoon into a greased 13"x9" baking pan. Bake at 350 degrees for one hour. Serves 4 to 6.

One-Dish Macaroni & Cheese

Carolyn Cote
Burlington, CT

So easy since the pasta isn't cooked first...allows plenty of time to relax before friends arrive!

14-oz. pkg. elbow macaroni,
   uncooked
4 c. shredded Cheddar cheese

2 10-3/4 oz. cans Cheddar
   cheese soup
3-1/2 c. milk

Combine all ingredients in a buttered 3-quart casserole dish; cover and bake at 350 degrees for one hour. Uncover and bake 20 additional minutes. Serves 8 to 10.

Save the memories! Be sure to take pictures at your gathering and send copies to friends as a thank-you for coming. Or use an instant camera and give pictures to guests on their way home.

Potluck Vegetable Casserole

Michelle Rooney
Gooseberry Patch

Be ready...your friends will surely request the recipe for this dish.

17-oz. can creamed corn
2 c. shredded Swiss cheese
10-3/4 oz. can cream of celery
  soup
17-oz. can corn, drained
10-oz. pkg. frozen cauliflower,
  cooked and drained

10-oz. pkg. frozen broccoli,
  cooked and drained
4-oz. can sliced mushrooms
2 T. butter, melted
1-1/2 c. bread crumbs

Combine creamed corn, cheese and soup; add corn, cauliflower,
broccoli and mushrooms. Spoon into an ungreased 12"x7" baking pan;
set aside. Mix butter and bread crumbs together; sprinkle over
vegetable mixture. Bake at 375 degrees for 30 to 35 minutes. Makes
8 servings.

No time to bake bread for company on their way? Dress up
store-bought refrigerated bread sticks in no time.
Separate bread stick dough and lay flat; brush with olive
oil and sprinkle sesame seeds and snipped parsley
over top. Holding ends of bread sticks, twist
2 times; bake as directed.

Baked Spinach Casserole

Karen Pilcher
Burleson, TX

If you like spinach, you'll love this recipe!

3 T. onion, grated
16-oz. pkg. sliced mushrooms
3 T. butter
3 T. all-purpose flour
2 t. salt
1/4 t. white pepper

1/4 t. nutmeg
2 c. whipping cream
2 10-oz. pkgs. frozen chopped
   spinach, thawed, drained
   and divided
3 T. shredded Swiss cheese

Sauté onion and mushrooms in butter for 5 minutes; blend in flour, salt, pepper and nutmeg. Gradually stir in cream; heat to boiling, stirring constantly. Remove from heat; set aside. Place half the spinach in a greased 13"x9" baking pan; cover with half the mushroom mixture. Repeat layers; sprinkle with cheese. Set pan in a larger pan filled with 1/2 inch water; bake at 325 degrees for 40 minutes. Serves 6 to 8.

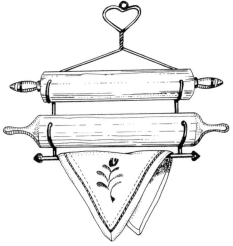

Cooking is at once child's play and adult joy.
And cooking done with care is an act of love.

- Craig Claiborne

Lemon Biscuits

Jennifer Licon-Conner
Gooseberry Patch

So light...wonderful with chicken, seafood and garden salads.

2 c. all-purpose flour
1 T. sugar
2 t. baking powder
2 t. lemon zest
1/2 t. baking soda

1/2 t. salt
1/2 c. shortening
1/3 c. buttermilk
1/3 c. mayonnaise

Combine first 6 ingredients in a mixing bowl; cut in shortening with a pastry cutter until coarse crumbs form. Make a well in the center; set aside. Whisk buttermilk and mayonnaise together; pour into well, stirring until just blended. Place dough on a lightly floured surface; knead until smooth, 10 to 12 times. Pat into a 1/2-inch thick rectangle; cut into biscuits using a round glass or biscuit cutter. Arrange on ungreased baking sheets; bake at 450 degrees until golden, 10 to 12 minutes. Cool slightly before serving. Makes 8 to 10.

Paper plates and cups don't have to be plain and boring. Look for those that come in bright colors, then quickly dress them up with ribbons, rick-rack, flowers or stickers.

Quick from the Cupboard Mains

Cheddar Ziti Bake

Wendy Lee Paffenroth
Pine Island, NY

This recipe is easily doubled...a handy dish to offer friends for open houses, graduations and receptions.

1-lb. pkg. sweet Italian sausages
1 lb. ground beef
1 onion, chopped
2 29-oz. cans crushed tomatoes

1 c. red wine or beef broth
1 T. Italian seasoning
16-oz. pkg. ziti pasta, cooked
4 c. shredded Cheddar cheese

Place sausages in a saucepan; cover with water. Boil for 15 to 20 minutes; drain and rinse under cold water. Cut into 1/2-inch slices; brown with ground beef in a 12" skillet. Add onion; sauté until tender. Add crushed tomatoes and wine or broth; stir in seasoning. Heat until boiling; reduce heat and simmer until thickened. Remove from heat; pour 1/4 cup sauce in the bottom of a roasting pan. Add half the pasta, half the remaining sauce and half the cheese. Repeat layers. Bake at 325 degrees until bubbly, about 40 minutes. Serves 8.

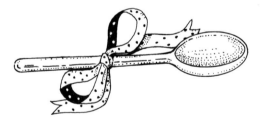

Delight dinner guests with a creative centerpiece. Stack several terra cotta pots, gluing inside each rim. Place floral foam inside the top pot and nestle a candle inside, then tuck small flowers around the candle base. Try making several in different heights and group together on the table.

Bowties & Blush Pasta Dish

Brooke Sottosanti
Columbia Station, OH

A restaurant-style meal in the comfort of your own home!

1 T. butter
1 onion, chopped
1 banana pepper, chopped
2 cloves garlic, chopped
1 T. all-purpose flour
3/4 c. milk
1/2 c. whipping cream

1/2 t. salt
1-1/4 c. spaghetti sauce
16-oz. pkg. bowtie pasta,
  cooked
1/4 c. grated Parmesan cheese
1/4 c. fresh basil, chopped

Melt butter over medium heat in a 12" skillet; add onion, pepper
and garlic. Sauté until tender; stir in flour. Gradually add milk, cream
and salt; bring to a boil. Mix in spaghetti sauce; heat for 10 minutes.
Remove from heat; pour into a serving bowl. Add pasta; mix gently.
Sprinkle with Parmesan cheese and basil; serve warm. Serves 8.

Use simple garnishes to dress up main dishes throughout
the year. Fresh mint sprigs add coolness and color to
summertime dishes while rosemary sprigs and
cranberries arranged to resemble holly add
a festive touch to holiday platters.

Oven-Baked Pineapple Pork Chops

Linda Patten
Lake Zurich, IL

*Any side dish goes well with this main...we like buttered noodles
sprinkled with Parmesan cheese.*

8-oz. can pineapple slices,
   drained with juice reserved
2 T. soy sauce
1/2 t. ground ginger
1/2 t. garlic powder

4 pork loin chops
1/3 c. Italian-seasoned bread
   crumbs
1 t. paprika

Combine 4 tablespoons pineapple juice, soy sauce, ginger and garlic
powder in a shallow bowl; add pork chops, turning once to coat.
Marinate in the refrigerator for at least 4 hours. Gently toss bread
crumbs and paprika in a pie pan; add pork chops, coating both sides.
Arrange pork chops in a shallow ungreased 13"x9" baking pan; bake
at 350 degrees for 25 minutes. Turn pork chops; place one pineapple
slice on each pork chop. Bake 25 additional minutes; serve warm.
Makes 4 servings.

Once you've planned a scrumptious menu for family &
friends, be sure to take notes...you're likely to want to
repeat it sometime down the road.

Pork Chop & Potato Bake

Lori Derham
Knoxville, IL

A simple dish with lots of flavor.

10-3/4 oz. can cream of celery
  soup
24-oz. pkg. frozen shredded
  hashbrowns, thawed
1/2 c. milk
1/2 c. sour cream
1/4 t. pepper

2.8-oz. can French fried onions,
  divided
6 pork chops, browned
1/2 t. seasoned salt
1 c. shredded Cheddar cheese,
  divided

Combine soup, hashbrowns, milk, sour cream, pepper and half
the French fried onions; spread into a buttered 13"x9" baking pan.
Arrange pork chops on top; sprinkle with seasoned salt. Cover with
aluminum foil; bake at 350 degrees for 40 minutes. Top with cheese
and remaining onions; bake, uncovered, 5 additional minutes.
Serves 6.

Add a warm glow to the party with a simple strand of
Lights. Decorate the table with a string of white lights
folded inside a sheer table runner or strip
of fabric. Sparkly!

Chicken Salad Croissants

Arlene Smulski
Lyons, IL

Great for a quick supper or a casual weekend lunch.

2 c. cooked chicken, cubed
1/3 c. celery, diced
1/4 c. raisins
1/4 c. dried cranberries
1/4 c. sliced almonds
2/3 c. mayonnaise
1/8 t. pepper

1 T. fresh parsley, minced
1 t. mustard
1 T. lemon juice
4 to 6 croissants, split in half
    horizontally
4 to 6 lettuce leaves

Combine the first 10 ingredients in a large mixing bowl; mix well. Cover and refrigerate for 2 to 3 hours. Spoon about 1/2 cup mixture on the bottom half of each croissant; add a lettuce leaf and the top croissant half. Makes 4 to 6.

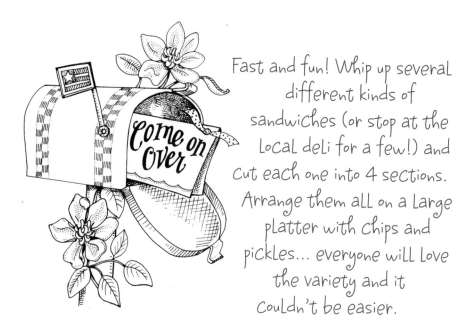

Fast and fun! Whip up several different kinds of sandwiches (or stop at the local deli for a few!) and cut each one into 4 sections. Arrange them all on a large platter with chips and pickles... everyone will love the variety and it couldn't be easier.

Quick from the Cupboard Mains

Santa Fe Sandwiches

Deanne Birkestrand
Minden, NE

Add a fresh fruit salad for a quick & tasty meal with friends.

6 hoagie buns, split in half
   horizontally
1/2 c. mayonnaise
1/2 c. sour cream
1/2 t. chili powder
1/2 t. cumin
1/4 t. salt
6 tomatoes, sliced
8-oz. pkg. sliced cooked turkey

1/2 c. sliced black olives
1/3 c. green onion, sliced
3 avocados, pitted, peeled and
   sliced
8-oz. pkg. shredded Cheddar
   cheese
Garnish: shredded lettuce and
   salsa

Arrange hoagie buns open-faced on an ungreased baking sheet; set aside. Mix the next 5 ingredients together; spread equally over hoagie buns. Layer remaining ingredients in the order listed equally on top of each bun; bake at 350 degrees for 15 minutes. Slice each in half to serve; garnish with lettuce and salsa. Makes 12 servings.

Wrap Santa Fe Sandwiches in parchment paper to keep them fresh before serving. Tie a gingham ribbon around each and tuck white daisies in the knots...guests will feel so special.

Fool-Proof Homemade Pizza

Vicki Vaughan
Franklin, MA

*My mother's specialty was homemade pizza. It took her about
10 hours to make and the slightest error would lead to disaster in the
kitchen! Through years of experimentation I now, thankfully, have the
easiest, fool-proof pizza recipe to share with family & friends!*

2 pkgs. active dry yeast
2 c. warm water
2 t. salt
6 T. olive oil

1 t. sugar
5 to 6 c. all-purpose flour,
    divided

Dissolve yeast in water; add salt, olive oil and sugar. Set aside until
foamy. Place 5 cups flour in a large mixing bowl; add yeast mixture.
Knead until a smooth dough forms, adding additional flour if
necessary; place in a well-greased bowl, turning to lightly coat sides
of dough. Cover and let rise in a warm place until double in bulk,
about one to 2 hours; divide into 2 equal portions. Pat into 2 greased
pizza pans; add toppings. Bake at 450 degrees for 10 minutes.
Makes 16 servings.

Toppings:

15-oz. can tomato sauce
1 t. sugar
1/4 c. grated Parmesan cheese
5 c. shredded mozzarella cheese
1 t. dried oregano

1 t. dried basil
Optional: sliced pepperoni, sliced
    mushrooms, sliced tomatoes
    and additional cheese

Combine tomato sauce and sugar; spread evenly over both crusts.
Sprinkle with remaining ingredients and any other desired toppings.

Quick from the Cupboard Mains

Crowd-Pleasing Potato Pizza

Marshall Williams
Westerville, OH

The slices disappear quickly!

3 potatoes, peeled and cubed
10-oz. tube refrigerated pizza
  crust
1/4 c. milk
1/2 t. salt
1-lb. pkg. bacon, diced
1 onion, chopped

1/2 c. red pepper, chopped
1-1/2 c. shredded Cheddar
  cheese
1-1/2 c. shredded mozzarella
  cheese
Optional: sour cream

Place potatoes in a large saucepan; barely cover with water. Boil until tender, about 20 to 25 minutes; drain and set aside. Flatten pizza dough on an ungreased 14" pizza pan; pinch edges to form a rim. Prick dough with a fork; bake at 350 degrees until golden, about 15 minutes. Cool on a wire rack. Transfer potatoes to a mixing bowl; add milk and salt. Mash until smooth; spread over crust. Slightly brown bacon; add onion and pepper and cook until tender. Drain and spread over potatoes. Sprinkle with cheeses; bake at 375 degrees for 20 minutes. Cut into wedges to serve; spread with sour cream, if desired. Makes 8 servings.

Have some fun at the dinner table. Cut out comic strips from the newspaper, laminate them, then use as napkin rings.

Potluck Casserole

Joan Macfarlane
Hillsboro, NH

Easy to make and yummy when reheated.

1 onion, chopped
1 green pepper, chopped
2 T. butter
1 lb. ground beef
16-oz. can whole tomatoes

1/2 c. long-cooking rice,
 uncooked
1-1/2 t. salt
1/2 t. pepper
1 t. chili powder

Sauté onion and green pepper in butter until tender; add ground beef. Brown; drain and remove from heat. Pour tomatoes in an ungreased 13"x9" baking pan; sprinkle with rice, salt, pepper and chili powder. Add ground beef mixture; stir to combine. Cover with aluminum foil; bake at 350 degrees for one hour. Serves 6.

Create a casserole topper. Unfold 2 refrigerated pie crusts; sprinkle one with pecans and sun-dried tomatoes (or any other goodies) and top with remaining crust. Roll crusts together and cut into shapes with cookie cutters. Bake at 425 degrees for 8 minutes and arrange on casserole before serving.

Saucy Meatloaf

Jennifer Inacio
York, PA

This has become a hit at informal dinner parties. I even made this for my friend who doesn't like meatloaf...she loved it so much, she asked for the recipe and she now makes it at least twice a month!

1-1/2 lbs. ground beef
1/2 c. quick-cooking oats,
    uncooked
1/2 c. onion, chopped

1-1/2 t. salt
1 t. pepper
1 c. tomato juice
1 egg

Combine all ingredients; mix well. Pat into an ungreased 9"x5" loaf pan; pour sauce on top. Bake at 350 degrees for 1-1/2 hours; let stand 5 minutes before slicing. Makes 8 servings.

Sauce:
Stir all ingredients together; mix well.

6-oz. can tomato sauce
3 T. vinegar
2 T. mustard

3 T. brown sugar, packed
2 t. Worcestershire sauce

My doctor told me to stop having intimate dinners for four.
Unless there are three other people.
– Orson Welles

Overnight Chicken Casserole

Cammi Kruse
Cosmos, MN

So easy because you don't have to cook the noodles!

2-1/2 c. cooked chicken, diced
2 c. elbow macaroni, uncooked
10-3/4 oz. can cream of chicken
   soup
1 c. plus 3 T. milk
14-1/2 oz. can chicken broth

8-oz. pkg. pasteurized processed
   cheese spread, cubed
1 t. salt
1 onion, chopped
1/4 c. celery, diced

Combine all ingredients together; spread in an ungreased
13"x9" baking pan. Cover with aluminum foil; refrigerate overnight.
Uncover and bake at 350 degrees for 1-1/2 hours. Serves 8.

Draw Here!

Kids coming for dinner too? Set up a separate table for
them and use a sheet of butcher paper for the tablecloth.
Place a flowerpot filled with markers, crayons and
stickers in the middle...they'll have a blast!

Feed-'Em-All Casserole

Tammy Rowe
Bellevue, OH

Expect ooh's and ahh's when you serve this hearty chicken dish.

3 boneless, skinless chicken
    breasts, cooked and cubed
16-oz. pkg. wide egg noodles,
    cooked
2 c. sour cream
15-oz. can mixed vegetables,
    drained

2-oz. jar pimentos, drained
1/4 c. grated Parmesan cheese
1 T. dried parsley, chopped
1 t. garlic powder
1/2 t. salt
1/2 t. pepper
2.8-oz. can French fried onions

Combine all ingredients, except French fried onions, in a large mixing
bowl; mix well. Spread in a buttered 13"x9" baking pan; bake at
350 degrees for 10 minutes. Sprinkle with French fried onions; bake
10 additional minutes or until bubbly and golden. Serves 8 to 10.

One-Skillet Chicken & Rice

Julie Heinze
Weston, OH

Clean up's a breeze!

1/4 c. all-purpose flour
1 T. seasoned salt
6 boneless, skinless chicken
    breasts
2 T. oil
2 14-1/2 oz. cans whole
    tomatoes, chopped

1-1/4 oz. pkg. taco seasoning
    mix
1 c. celery, chopped
1 c. long-cooking rice, uncooked
1/2 c. onion, chopped
1/2 c. parsley, chopped

Combine flour and seasoned salt in a plastic zipping bag; add chicken,
shaking to coat. Brown chicken in oil in a 12" skillet; add tomatoes,
taco seasoning, celery, rice and onion. Bring to a boil; reduce heat,
cover and simmer for 20 minutes. Sprinkle with parsley. Serves 6.

Sour Cream Taco Bake

Sheri Cazier
Black Diamond, WA

My husband always requests this special dish for his birthday.

1-1/2 lbs. ground beef
1-1/4 c. onion, chopped and
   divided
1-1/4 oz. pkg. taco seasoning
   mix
12-oz. can diced tomatoes
2 T. salsa

1/2 c. oil
12 corn tortillas
4 c. shredded Monterey Jack
   cheese
2 c. sour cream
1 t. seasoned salt
pepper to taste

Sauté ground beef and 1/2 cup onion until beef is browned; drain. Add taco seasoning mix, tomatoes and salsa; reduce heat and simmer for 20 minutes. Set aside to cool. Heat oil in 12" skillet; add tortillas, one at a time, heating on both sides until just soft. Drain on paper towels; set aside. Spoon 2 tablespoons meat sauce, 2 tablespoons cheese and 2 tablespoons remaining onion in the center of each tortilla; fold in half and arrange in a greased 13"x9" baking pan. Spread any remaining meat sauce, cheese and onion on top; set aside. Combine sour cream and seasoned salt; spread over tacos. Sprinkle with pepper; bake at 325 degrees for 25 to 30 minutes. Makes 12 servings.

Clever Condiments! When serving Mexican meals, slice the tops off peppers, rinse and remove seeds. Then fill with guacamole, sour cream and salsa. Cover with reserved tops and refrigerate until ready to serve. Works great for Cookouts too...fill with mustard, mayo and Catsup.

Black Bean Spaghetti Sauce

Cyndy Rogers
Upton, MA

Spoon over a heaping plate of warm spaghetti noodles.

1 onion, sliced
1 red pepper, sliced
1 yellow pepper, sliced
8-oz. pkg. sliced mushrooms
14-1/2 oz. can diced tomatoes

15-oz. can black beans, drained
  and rinsed
3-1/2 oz. jar capers, packed in
  water
2 t. dried Italian seasoning

Sauté the first 4 ingredients until crisp-tender in a 12" skillet sprayed with non-stick vegetable spray over medium-high heat; stir constantly. Add remaining ingredients; bring to a boil. Reduce heat and simmer for 15 minutes; stir frequently. Makes 6 servings.

Use old serving dishes in a new way for a fresh look.
Handed-down cream and sugar sets can hold sauces,
bread sticks can be arranged in gravy boats and a trifle
dish can make a great salad bowl.

Bubble Pizza

Tracy Lindberg
Meridian, ID

So fun to make for a house full of young guests!

3 7-1/2 oz. tubes refrigerated buttermilk biscuits, quartered
14-oz. jar spaghetti sauce, divided
3 c. shredded mozzarella cheese, divided

1 clove garlic, minced
Optional: sliced pepperoni, sliced mushrooms, onion, ham, sausage or pineapple

Place biscuit pieces in a large mixing bowl; add half the spaghetti sauce, 2 cups cheese and garlic. Mix until biscuit pieces are well coated; spread in a greased 13"x9" baking pan. Pour remaining sauce on top; add any optional toppings. Sprinkle with remaining cheese; bake at 350 degrees for 40 to 45 minutes. Serves 8 to 10.

You don't have to spend a lot of time setting the table for casual gatherings. Just wrap colorful napkins around silverware and slip them into a glass at each place setting. It's so charming...and you don't have to remember where the forks, knives and spoons go!

Simple Stuffed Shells

Max Bentley
Waunakee, WI

A 3-cheese delight!

24-oz. carton cottage cheese
1/4 c. grated Parmesan cheese
1 t. garlic powder
2 eggs
salt and pepper to taste
12-oz. pkg. large shell pasta,
    uncooked

1 c. spinach leaves, torn
14-oz. can diced Italian
    tomatoes
14-oz. jar spaghetti sauce
2 c. shredded mozzarella cheese

Combine the first 5 ingredients in a medium mixing bowl; mix well.
Spoon into shells; arrange in a 13"x9" baking pan sprayed with
non-stick vegetable spray. Tuck spinach between shells; pour tomatoes
and spaghetti sauce on top, making sure all shells are well covered.
Cover with aluminum foil; bake at 375 degrees for 30 minutes.
Uncover and sprinkle with mozzarella cheese; bake 15 additional
minutes or until cheese is melted. Serves 6.

Sophistication in a snap! Fill 3 stemmed glasses half full
with water, float a tea light in each and group them
together in the center of the table.

Slow-Cooker Steak

Vickie Simpson
Norfolk, VA

The aroma will bring family & friends to the table in no time!

3 potatoes, peeled and quartered
4-oz. pkg. baby carrots
2 stalks celery, diced
1 onion, chopped
6 beef round steaks, browned
12-oz. jar beef gravy

10-3/4 oz. can cream of
   mushroom soup
1/8 t. curry powder
1/8 t. garlic salt
1/8 t. pepper

Combine vegetables; place in a slow cooker. Arrange steaks on top; set aside. Mix remaining ingredients together; pour over steaks, stirring to coat vegetables and steaks. Heat on low setting for 6 to 8 hours or on high for 3 to 4 hours. Serves 6.

Guests are sure to head to the powder room to wash up before dinner, so why not offer them individual handtowels. Just roll up small white washcloths and tuck them all in a pretty basket by the sink. They'll love the pampering!

Meatball Sub Casserole

Mary Kowaleski
Shawano, WI

All the yum of subs in one easy dish.

1/3 c. green onion, chopped
1/4 c. seasoned bread crumbs
3 T. grated Parmesan cheese
1 lb. ground beef
1-lb. loaf Italian bread, cut into
    one-inch thick slices
8-oz. pkg. cream cheese,
    softened

1/2 c. mayonnaise
1 t. Italian seasoning
1/4 t. pepper
2 c. shredded mozzarella
    cheese, divided
28-oz. jar spaghetti sauce
1 c. water
2 cloves garlic, minced

Combine onion, bread crumbs and Parmesan cheese in a large bowl; mix in ground beef. Shape mixture into one-inch meatballs; place in an ungreased jelly-roll pan and bake at 400 degrees for 15 to 20 minutes. Arrange bread slices in a single layer in a greased 13"x9" baking dish; set aside. Combine cream cheese, mayonnaise, Italian seasoning and pepper; spread over bread. Sprinkle with 1/2 cup mozzarella cheese. Combine sauce, water, garlic and meatballs; spread over cheese mixture. Sprinkle remaining mozzarella on top; bake at 350 degrees for 30 minutes. Serves 6 to 8.

No tablecloth? No problem! It's absolutely optional, so go without...or use creative tabletoppers like an old-fashioned quilt, favorite scarf or lengths of lace.

Reuben Casserole

Peggy Zahrt
Estherville, IA

The classic sandwich becomes a casserole.

16-oz. jar sauerkraut, drained
6 to 9 oz. corned beef slices,
   chopped
1-1/2 c. shredded Swiss cheese
1/2 c. mayonnaise

1/4 c. Thousand Island salad
   dressing
6 T. butter, melted
4 to 6 slices rye bread, cubed

Layer sauerkraut, beef and cheese in an ungreased 13"x9" baking pan; set aside. Combine mayonnaise and Thousand Island salad dressing; spread over cheese layer. Drizzle butter on top; sprinkle with bread cubes. Bake at 350 degrees for 30 minutes or until cheese is bubbly. Serves 6.

Dress up a one-dish dinner when serving on individual plates. A simple chopped herb around the edge of the plate will add a lot of color, and a complementary sauce that has been drizzled around the edge will give a nice frame to the meal. Your guests will think you've had dinner catered!

Quick from the Cupboard Mains

Quick Ham & Cheeses

Rosemarie Wasko
Portage, PA

Serve with tomato soup...ultimate comfort food!

2 12-oz. tubes refrigerated
   biscuits
5-oz. can minced ham
1 t. dried, minced onion

1 t. margarine
5 slices Swiss cheese
2 T. butter, melted
1 t. poppy seed

Flatten each biscuit; arrange 5 on an aluminum foil-lined baking sheet, setting remaining biscuits to the side. Combine ham, onion and margarine together; spread equally over 5 biscuits. Arrange one slice Swiss cheese on top of each; place remaining biscuits on top of cheese. Pinch top and bottom biscuits together to seal. Brush with butter; sprinkle with poppy seed. Bake at 350 degrees until golden, about 15 to 18 minutes. Makes 5 servings.

Ham & Swiss Pie

Mary Rita Schlagel
Warwick, NY

Breakfast, lunch or dinner...this pie is a treat!

2 c. cooked ham, diced
1 c. shredded Swiss cheese
1/3 c. onion, chopped
4 eggs, beaten

2 c. milk
1 c. biscuit baking mix
pepper, paprika and dried
   parsley to taste

Spread ham, cheese and onion in the bottom of an ungreased 9" deep-dish pie pan; set aside. Place eggs, milk and biscuit baking mix into a blender; mix for 15 seconds. Pour over ham mixture; sprinkle with remaining ingredients. Bake at 400 degrees for 30 to 40 minutes or until a knife inserted in the center removes clean; cool for 10 minutes before serving. Serves 6.

Chicken Casserole Supreme

Carol Rickard
Chardon, OH

You can't go wrong with this popular dish.

1 onion, chopped
1 c. green pepper, chopped
2 T. butter
16-oz. pkg. chicken-flavored
    stuffing mix
4 c. chicken broth

6 eggs, beaten
3 10-3/4 oz. cans cream of
    celery soup
8 c. cooked chicken, chopped
3 c. prepared rice

Sauté onion and green pepper in butter; set aside. Combine stuffing mix and broth in a very large mixing bowl or roaster; stir in eggs, soup, chicken, rice, onion and green pepper. Divide evenly between 2 lightly buttered 13"x9" baking pans; bake at 325 degrees for 30 to 40 minutes. Serves 16.

Everyone will love making toasts with these cute beverage charms. Pick up several small bells in different colors at a local craft store. Thread 2 or 3 onto ribbon and tie to stemmed glasses.

Chicken in Cream Sauce

Louise Denton
Sacramento, CA

Every bite is moist and juicy!

8 boneless, skinless chicken breasts
1.05-oz. pkg. Italian salad dressing mix, divided
8-oz. pkg. cream cheese, softened and divided

10-3/4 oz. can cream of mushroom soup
1/2 c. green onion, chopped
1/3 c. white wine or chicken broth

Arrange chicken in a greased 2-quart baking pan; set aside. Heat half the package Italian dressing mix, half the package cream cheese and soup together in a microwave-safe bowl, stirring until well blended; set remaining mix and cream cheese aside for use in another recipe. Stir onion and wine or broth into cream cheese mixture; spread over chicken breasts. Bake at 350 degrees for one hour or until juices run clear when chicken is pierced with a fork. Makes 8 servings.

A special touch when serving seafood. Wrap lemon halves in cheesecloth, tie with a colorful ribbon, attach a placecard, if desired, and set one on each plate. Guests can squeeze the lemon over their dishes...the cheesecloth prevents squirting and catches seeds!

Scalloped Scallops

Cheryl Kiss
Kingsport, TN

A sure-fire winner!

3/4 c. butter, melted
2 c. round buttery crackers,
  crushed
1 c. bread crumbs
1-1/2 lbs. scallops, divided

1-1/2 c. half-and-half, divided
salt and pepper to taste
2 t. paprika
Garnish: 1 lemon, sliced into
  4 to 6 wedges

Combine butter, crushed cracker crumbs and bread crumbs; mix well. Sprinkle one-third in the bottom of a buttered 1-1/2 quart casserole dish; top with half the scallops. Pour on half the cream; salt and pepper to taste. Repeat layers; top with remaining bread crumb mixture. Sprinkle with paprika; bake at 350 degrees until scallops are heated through, about 30 to 40 minutes. Spoon onto serving plates; garnish each with a lemon wedge. Makes 4 to 6 servings.

Give a rose to everyone at the table! Unfold a green napkin and lay it across a drinking glass. Roll up a white napkin (pink looks pretty too) and slip it into the glass, so the green napkin comes up over the edges, and the white "rose" can be seen in the middle.

Citrus-Cherry Pork & Pasta

Brad Daugherty
Gooseberry Patch

Guests are always excited when this dish is on the menu.

1 t. oil
1 lb. pork tenderloin, cubed
1/2 sweet onion, sliced
2 T. orange juice
2 T. balsamic vinegar
2 T. olive oil
1/4 t. salt

1/4 t. pepper
1 T. orange zest
8-oz. pkg. mostaccioli pasta,
   cooked and drained
3 c. broccoli flowerets
1/2 c. dried cherries
1/2 c. chopped walnuts

Heat oil over medium-high heat in a 12" non-stick skillet. Add pork and onion; sauté 3 to 4 minutes or until pork is browned and onion is tender; set aside. Shake orange juice, vinegar, olive oil, salt, pepper and orange zest in a small jar with a tight fitting lid; set aside. Toss pork and onion mixture, pasta, broccoli, cherries and walnuts together in a large serving bowl; pour orange juice mixture on top. Gently toss; serve immediately. Makes 6 servings.

Dinners at home don't have to be in the kitchen...and the outdoors isn't reserved for cookouts. Bake up a tasty dish inside, then lead everyone to the backyard to dine al fresco...they'll be so surprised!

So-Tender Barbecue Chicken

Christina Jones
Lebanon, TN

We pour any extra barbecue sauce over prepared rice for a speedy side.

4 boneless, skinless chicken
   breasts
1/2 c. catsup
1/4 c. vinegar
1/4 c. Worcestershire sauce
1/2 c. water

6 T. butter
2 t. salt
1/2 c. brown sugar, packed
2 t. dry mustard
2 t. paprika
1 t. chili powder

Place chicken in an ungreased 13"x9" baking pan; set aside. Mix remaining ingredients together; spread over chicken. Bake at 300 degrees for 2 hours or until juices run clear when chicken is pierced with a fork. Serves 4.

Oven-Crispy Barbecue Chicken

Margie Williams
Gooseberry Patch

Team up with cornbread and a crisp salad for a pleasing dinner.

18-oz. bottle barbecue sauce
4 to 6 boneless, skinless chicken
   breasts
4 c. crispy rice cereal, crushed
1 t. salt

1 t. pepper
1 t. garlic powder
1 t. onion powder
1 t. dried parsley

Pour barbecue sauce in a bowl; coat both sides of chicken breasts with sauce. Set aside. Combine remaining ingredients; roll chicken breasts in mixture. Lay on an aluminum foil-lined baking sheet; bake at 400 degrees for 30 minutes. Serves 4 to 6.

Salisbury Steak & Onion Gravy

Dawn Lawrence
Claremont, NH

It won't last long!

10-1/2 oz. can French onion
   soup, divided
1-1/2 lbs. ground beef
1/2 c. bread crumbs
1 egg, beaten
1/4 t. salt

1/8 t. pepper
1 T. all-purpose flour
1/4 c. catsup
1/4 c. water
1 t. Worcestershire sauce
1/2 t. mustard

Combine 1/2 cup soup, beef, bread crumbs, egg, salt and pepper in a
large mixing bowl; shape into 6 patties. Brown in a skillet; drain and
set aside. Gradually blend remaining soup with flour until smooth; add
remaining ingredients. Pour into skillet; stir well. Cover; return to heat
and simmer for 20 minutes, stirring occasionally. Serves 6.

Hand-written menus lend a
personal touch to any table.
Cut colored papers to fit the
front of old-fashioned milk bottles
or Mason jars. Write on details and
wrap around the jars with a
pretty ribbon...fill jars with
water and flowers and arrange
in the center of the table.

Rose Hill Chicken Spaghetti

Aliceson Haynes
Orange, TX

Serve up spaghetti in a whole new way...you'll be
pleasantly surprised!

1 onion, chopped
2 stalks celery, chopped
1/4 c. margarine
14-1/2 oz. can tomatoes with
  green chile peppers
10-3/4 oz. can cream of chicken
  soup
10-3/4 oz. can cream of
  mushroom soup

8-oz. pkg. pasteurized
  processed cheese spread,
  cubed
4-1/2 oz. can mushrooms,
  drained
seasoned salt to taste
4 boneless, skinless chicken
  breasts, boiled and chopped
12-oz. pkg. spaghetti, cooked

Sauté onion and celery in margarine until tender in a large stockpot;
add tomatoes, soups, cheese and mushrooms. Simmer until cheese
melts; sprinkle with salt. Add chicken; stir well. Simmer until heated
through; stir in spaghetti. Serves 8 to 10.

Cooking Rule: If at first you don't succeed,
order pizza.
– Unknown

Classic Lasagna

Naomi Cooper
Delaware, OH

Best when assembled the day before and refrigerated overnight.

2 lbs. ground beef
1 onion, chopped
2 cloves garlic, chopped
2-1/2 t. salt
1/4 t. pepper
1/2 t. dried basil
1 T. dried parsley
2 bay leaves
2 6-oz. cans tomato paste

1-1/2 c. hot water
2 c. cottage cheese
2 eggs, beaten
16-oz. pkg. lasagna noodles,
  cooked and divided
4 c. shredded mozzarella cheese,
  divided
1/4 c. grated Parmesan cheese

Brown beef, onion and garlic in a 12" skillet; season with salt, pepper, basil, parsley and bay leaves. Stir in tomato paste and hot water; bring to a boil. Reduce heat; simmer for 5 minutes. In a separate bowl, blend cottage cheese with eggs; set aside. Spread a thin layer of beef mixture in a greased 13"x9" baking pan; top with a layer of noodles. Spread half the cottage cheese mixture over noodles; sprinkle with half the cheese. Repeat layers; sprinkle with Parmesan cheese. Cover with aluminum foil; bake at 350 degrees for 30 to 45 minutes. Serves 8.

Brush hot glue on the sides of tea lights and decorate with buttons, ribbon, beads, small shells or hard candies. Arrange on a pedestal plate for a centerpiece or dance along the mantel...decorating is done!

Super Scrumptious Soft Tacos

Tina Stidam
Delaware, OH

Try these with crunchy taco shells too!

1 lb. ground beef
2/3 c. water
1 T. chili powder
1/2 t. salt
1/4 t. garlic powder
1/4 t. cayenne pepper
15-1/2 oz. can kidney beans,
    drained

1 head lettuce, torn
1 c. Cheddar cheese, shredded
2/3 c. olives, sliced
2 tomatoes, chopped
1 onion, chopped
8 10-inch flour tortillas
Garnish: avocado and sour
    cream

Brown ground beef in a 12" skillet, stirring occasionally; drain. Stir in
water, chili powder, salt, garlic powder, cayenne pepper and kidney
beans. Heat to boiling; reduce heat and simmer for 15 minutes, stirring
occasionally. Remove from heat; set aside to cool for 10 minutes. Toss
lettuce, cheese, olives, tomatoes and onion in large bowl. Spoon beef
mixture down the centers of the tortillas; sprinkle with lettuce mixture.
Garnish with avocado and sour cream. Serves 8.

Host a bring-your-favorite-topping taco party. Just provide
the shells and the beef or chicken and everyone else can
bring lettuce, tomatoes, olives, cheese, onion, salsa,
sour cream and guacamole. Delicious!

Quick from the Cupboard Mains

Chicken Enchiladas

Michele Nance
Stevenson, WA

Add diced green chiles to enchiladas for extra zip!

28-oz. can green enchilada
    sauce
10-3/4 oz. can cream of chicken
    soup
2 c. sour cream
2-1/2 lbs. boneless, skinless
    chicken breasts, boiled and
    chopped

20 flour tortillas
4 c. shredded Colby Jack cheese,
    divided
4 c. shredded Cheddar cheese,
    divided

Mix sauce, soup and sour cream together; spread one-third in an ungreased 13"x9" baking pan. Mix one-third with chicken; spoon onto tortillas and sprinkle with half the cheeses. Roll up jelly-roll style; place seam-side down on sauce. Spread with remaining sauce and cheeses; bake, covered, at 375 degrees for 20 minutes. Uncover and bake 10 additional minutes. Makes 20 servings.

Taco Pie Delight

Tina White
Charleston, IL

This hearty south-of-the-border bake is popular with everyone.

1 lb. ground beef, browned
1-1/4 oz. pkg. taco seasoning
16-oz. can refried beans
2 c. shredded mozzarella and
    Cheddar cheese mix

8-oz. jar taco sauce
9-inch pie crust, baked
1 tomato, chopped
Garnish: shredded lettuce,
    sour cream

Combine ground beef and taco seasoning mix together in a skillet; simmer. Add refried beans; heat through. Layer ground beef mixture, cheese and taco sauce in the pie crust. Bake at 350 degrees for 15 minutes; sprinkle with tomato. Slice into wedges; top with desired garnishes before serving. Makes 8 servings.

Better-than-Ever Beef Stroganoff
Trisha MacQueen
Bakersfield, CA

You only need one skillet to whip up this favorite.

1-1/2 lbs. round steak, sliced
1/4 c. all-purpose flour
pepper to taste
1/2 c. butter
4-oz. can sliced mushrooms, drained
1/2 c. onion, chopped

1 clove garlic, minced
10-1/2 oz. can beef broth
10-3/4 oz. can cream of mushroom soup
1 c. sour cream
6-oz. pkg. medium egg noodles, cooked

Coat steak with flour; sprinkle with pepper. Brown in a 12" skillet with butter; add mushrooms, onion and garlic. Sauté until tender; stir in broth. Reduce heat; cover and simmer for one hour. Blend in soup and sour cream; heat on low for about 5 minutes. Do not boil. Spoon over warm noodles to serve. Serves 4.

Bring a whole new look to your table with a table runner you can make in a flash. Just tie 5 oversized cloth napkins together, corner-to-corner, and lay across the table.

Beef Stir-Fry with Couscous

Vickie Burns
Norwich, OH

No one's ever late for dinner when this is being served!

1-1/4 lb. boneless beef top
    sirloin steak
14-1/2 oz. can beef broth
1 c. couscous, uncooked
1 T. olive oil
1 red pepper, sliced

1/2 c. sweet onion, chopped
1 clove garlic, minced
1/2 c. honey Dijon barbecue
    sauce
1 T. fresh parsley, chopped

Cut steak lengthwise in half and then crosswise into 1/4-inch thick strips; set aside. Bring beef broth to a boil in a medium saucepan; stir in couscous. Cover; remove from heat. Heat oil over medium-high heat in a 12" non-stick skillet until hot; add half the beef. Stir-fry one to 2 minutes or until outside surface is no longer pink; remove. Repeat with remaining steak. In same skillet, stir-fry red pepper, onion and garlic for 2 to 3 minutes. Return beef to skillet; stir in barbecue sauce. Heat and stir one to 2 additional minutes or until heated through. Spoon over couscous to serve; sprinkle with parsley. Makes 4 servings.

So fun with an oriental dinner! Place a 6"x6" tile next to each guest's place and rest chopsticks on top...just be sure to have forks available too!

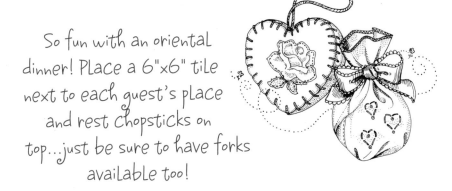

Easy-on-the-Cook Barbecue Ribs

Deb Bleick
Woodstock, GA

Be sure to have lots of napkins handy!

3 lbs. country-style pork ribs,
   browned
1/2 c. catsup
1-1/2 t. salt
1/8 t. chili powder
1/2 t. dry mustard

2 T. brown sugar, packed
2 10-3/4 oz. cans tomato soup
1 T. Worcestershire sauce
1/4 c. vinegar
1 onion, diced
1 T. lemon juice

Place ribs in large roasting pan; set aside. Combine remaining ingredients; mix well. Stir in one to 2 cups water; pour over ribs. Bake at 350 degrees until tender, about 2 to 3 hours. Serves 6.

Look beyond traditional napkins when hosting family & friends. Try using bandannas, colorful dishtowels, inexpensive fabrics from the craft store or, for especially saucy foods, use moistened washcloths...they'll love it!

Quick from the Cupboard Mains

Pantry Ham

Rosalia Burns
Delafield, WI

I remember how excited I was when my mother made this ham because it meant we were having company...and also one of her fabulous desserts!

8-lb. cooked ham with bone
4 12-oz. cans cola
2 15-1/4 oz. cans pineapple
    juice
1 T. whole cloves
1 c. brown sugar, packed

3 to 4 T. Dijon mustard
20-oz. can sliced pineapple,
    drained
6-oz. jar maraschino cherries,
    drained

Place ham, cola and pineapple juice in a large stockpot; simmer until ham is thoroughly warmed and the liquid is almost gone. Place ham in a large roaster; slice diamond cuts on top. Insert whole cloves in each diamond; set aside. Mix brown sugar and mustard together; rub over ham. Arrange pineapple rings and cherries over ham, keeping in place with toothpicks if necessary. Add juices from stockpot; bake at 350 degrees until warmed through, about 1-1/2 hours. Occasionally baste with juices; slice and serve. Serves 8 to 10.

Make-It-&-Go Ham Dinner

Kimber Bowersox
Morristown, TN

Simple and pleasing.

3 to 5-lb. smoked ham with
    bone

2 12-oz. cans cola
1 c. brown sugar, packed

Place ham in a slow cooker; set aside. Combine cola and brown sugar; pour over ham. Heat on high setting for 2-1/2 hours; baste occasionally. Serves 6.

Traditional Sunday Steak

Kathy Rudd
Lake Worth, FL

Sure to impress everyone at the table!

1-1/2 lb. beef flank steak
2 T. all-purpose flour
2 T. olive oil
salt and pepper to taste
1 cube beef bouillon

1 c. water
2 T. fresh parsley, chopped
1 t. sugar
3/4 t. dried thyme

Score steak on one side; coat both sides with flour. Place in a skillet with oil; heat until browned, turning to brown both sides. Season with salt and pepper; add bouillon, water, parsley, sugar and thyme. Cover; simmer for 1-1/2 to 2 hours or until beef is tender. Serve with steak gravy. Serves 4.

Steak Gravy:

pan juices
3 T. all-purpose flour

1/2 t. browning and seasoning
  sauce

Add water to pan juices to equal a total of 1-1/4 cups liquid; return to skillet and set aside. Whisk flour and 1/2 cup water together until smooth; gradually pour into pan juices, heating over low heat. Add browning sauce; stir and heat until thick and bubbly.

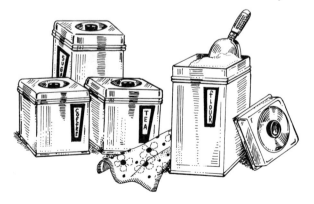

Quick from the Cupboard Mains

Baked Herb Chicken

Susan Young
Madison, AL

A quick & easy, one-pan meal.

6 boneless, skinless chicken
   breasts
1 c. fresh parsley, chopped
1/2 c. grated Parmesan cheese

1/2 c. chopped pecans
1/3 c. oil
3 T. lemon juice
3 T. dried basil

Arrange chicken in a greased 13"x9" baking pan; set aside. Combine remaining ingredients; pour over chicken. Bake at 350 degrees for 45 to 50 minutes. Serves 6.

Tomato-Olive Pasta

Donna Weidner
St. Augustine, FL

Be sure to make enough for extra helpings!

3 cloves garlic, minced
2 T. olive oil
1/3 c. sun-dried tomatoes,
   chopped
1-1/4 c. chicken broth

1/2 c. black olives, chopped
1/2 c. fresh parsley, chopped
16-oz. pkg. penne pasta, cooked
1 c. crumbled feta cheese

Sauté garlic in olive oil over medium heat for 30 seconds; add sun-dried tomatoes and chicken broth. Simmer for 10 minutes; stir in black olives and parsley. Pour tomato mixture over pasta; top with cheese, tossing lightly. Makes 8 servings.

Chicken with Basil Cream Sauce

*Elaine Slabinski
Monroe Twp, NJ*

*Whipping cream and Parmesan cheese add extra richness
to this easy chicken dish.*

1/4 c. milk
1/4 c. bread crumbs
4 boneless, skinless chicken
    breasts
3 T. butter
1 T. olive oil
1/2 c. chicken broth

1 c. whipping cream
4-oz. jar pimentos, drained
1/2 c. grated Parmesan cheese
1/4 c. fresh basil, minced
1/8 t. pepper
1 t. cornstarch

Place milk and bread crumbs in separate bowls; dip chicken in milk,
then coat with bread crumbs. Melt butter and oil in a skillet; add
chicken. Heat until browned; remove from pan. Place in oven to keep
warm. Pour broth in skillet; bring to a boil. Stir in cream and pimentos;
boil and stir for one minute. Reduce heat; mix in Parmesan, basil
and pepper. Cook until heated through; add cornstarch, stirring until
thickened. Pour over chicken before serving. Serves 4.

So quick & easy! Use
empty seed packs to hold
silverware...cut off the tops
of packets with pinking shears,
empty the seeds then slide the
silverware handles inside.

Quick from the Cupboard Mains

Mom's Stuffed Cabbage Rolls

Megan Pepping
Coshocton, OH

Every year we look forward to Fall when we get the huge heads of cabbage that have the perfect leaves for these rolls.

3 qts. plus 1/2 c. water, divided
3-1/2 lb. head cabbage
1 lb. ground beef
1/2 c. instant rice, uncooked
1 onion, minced
2 eggs, beaten
1 c. mushrooms, chopped
2 t. salt, divided

1/8 t. pepper
1/8 t. allspice
1 onion, sliced into rings
1/4 t. salt
16-oz. can tomato sauce
28-oz. can tomatoes
1/3 c. lemon juice
1/4 c. brown sugar, packed

Bring 3 quarts water to a boil in a large stockpot; add cabbage leaves and simmer 2 to 3 minutes or until leaves are pliable. Remove cabbage and drain. Place 12 of the largest leaves to the side. Combine beef, rice, onion, eggs, mushrooms, one teaspoon salt, pepper, allspice and 1/4 cup water; mix until well blended. Place 1/4 cup beef mixture into the center of each leaf; roll up beginning at the thick end of each leaf. Place a few remaining cabbage leaves in bottom of a Dutch oven; arrange rolls seam-side down on leaves and top with sliced onions. In a large mixing bowl, combine remaining salt, tomato sauce, tomatoes, lemon juice and remaining water together; pour over cabbage rolls. Bring to a boil over medium heat; sprinkle with brown sugar. Remove from heat; cover and bake at 350 degrees for 1-1/2 hours. Uncover and bake for 1-1/2 additional hours. Serves 12.

If you're planning on serving cold beverages with the main dish, put some freezer-proof cups in the freezer a few hours before guests arrive...a chilled glass makes all the difference!

Deluxe Chicken Bake

Lisa Peterson
Sabina, OH

Easy to make and always a hit!

8-oz. pkg. wide egg noodles,
   cooked
10 T. butter, divided
3-1/2 c. milk, divided
1/4 c. all-purpose flour
1/2 t. salt
1/8 t. pepper

2 10-oz. cans chicken gravy
4 c. cooked chicken, diced
2 T. pimento
1/2 c. seasoned bread crumbs
1/2 to 1 c. shredded Cheddar
   cheese

Combine noodles, 2 tablespoons butter and 1/2 cup milk; set aside.
Mix 6 tablespoons butter, flour, salt and pepper in a heavy saucepan;
heat and stir until smooth. Pour in remaining milk, whisking until
thickened; add gravy, chicken and pimento. Stir in noodles; remove
from heat. Spread into a greased 13"x9" baking pan; bake, covered, at
350 degrees for 25 minutes. Melt remaining butter; mix in bread
crumbs and cheese. Sprinkle over noodle mixture. Bake, uncovered,
for an additional 10 minutes. Serves 6.

Pick up inexpensive, glass salt & pepper shakers at flea
markets. Dress them up by gluing on rhinestones or colorful
beads. For the holidays, tie on a couple jingle
bells...they'll ring with each shake!

Elegant Chicken Roll-Ups

Teri Lindquist
Gurnee, IL

Just right for a special occasion.

8 boneless, skinless chicken
   breasts
8 slices cooked ham
8 slices Swiss cheese
10-3/4 oz. can cream of chicken
   soup
1/2 c. dry white wine or chicken
   broth

1/2 c. sour cream
1 t. dried tarragon
1 t. pepper
2 c. cornbread stuffing mix,
   crushed
1 t. dried parsley

Wrap each chicken breast in a slice of ham; arrange in a greased 13"x9" baking dish. Lay one slice cheese over each chicken breast; set aside. Whisk together soup, wine or broth, sour cream, tarragon and pepper; pour over chicken. Cover with aluminum foil; bake at 325 degrees for 40 minutes. Remove foil; baste chicken. Sprinkle with stuffing mix and parsley; bake, uncovered, for 15 additional minutes. Serves 8.

It's easy to make eye-catching floral arrangements by using unexpected containers. Instead of vases, try standing flowers in jars of water, then tuck the jars into simple paper shopping bags, formal top hats, or vintage purses.

Pizza Pasta Casserole

Maureen Rose
Lancaster, OH

Add any extra pizza toppings before sprinkling with cheese.

2 lbs. ground beef
1 onion, chopped
2 28-oz. jars spaghetti sauce
16-oz. pkg. spiral pasta, cooked

4 c. shredded mozzarella cheese,
  divided
8-oz. pkg. sliced pepperoni,
  divided

Brown ground beef with onion; drain. Stir in spaghetti sauce and pasta; spread equally in 2 greased 13"x9" baking pans. Sprinkle both with cheese; arrange pepperoni slices on tops. Bake at 350 degrees for 25 to 30 minutes. Makes 24 servings.

Host a progressive dinner with several friends. Each family serves one course at their house, as everyone travels from home to home. Start one place for appetizers, move to the next for soups and salads, again for the main dish and end with dessert!

Company Spaghetti Bake

Louann Rossman
Erie, PA

This dish reminds me of special visits to my grandparents' house when I was a young girl. It seems like we had this all the time...it's no wonder because it's so delicious and great to make ahead.

1 lb. ground beef
3/4 c. onion, finely chopped
1/2 c. green pepper, finely
   chopped
10-3/4 oz. can cream of
   mushroom soup
10-3/4 oz. can tomato soup

1-1/3 c. water
8-oz. can tomato sauce
1/2 t. salt
1 clove garlic, minced
8-oz. pkg. spaghetti, cooked
1-1/2 c. sharp Cheddar cheese,
   shredded and divided

Brown beef with onion and green pepper in a 12" skillet; drain. Add soups, water, tomato sauce, salt and garlic; simmer until heated through. Place spaghetti in a large mixing bowl; add sauce mixture and one cup cheese, mixing well. Spread into a greased 13"x9" baking pan; top with remaining cheese. Bake at 350 degrees for 45 minutes or until bubbly in center. Serves 6 to 8.

Out-of-town guests coming for the weekend? Make them feel at home by preparing a basket filled with in-season fresh fruit, snacks for late-night nibbles along with a local map and directions to favorite sites, shops and restaurants.

Beef & Sausage Empanada

Cheryl Lochmann
Powell, OH

A Mexican version of the Italian calzone that is sure to please family & friends. Make it up to 2 days in advance and refrigerate until baking.

1 lb. ground sausage
1 lb. ground beef
16-oz. jar medium salsa
3 c. shredded Cheddar cheese, divided
2 c. sour cream

1/4 t. cayenne pepper
1/2 t. cumin
6 10-inch flour tortillas, divided
29-oz. can enchilada sauce, divided
2 4-oz. cans green chiles

Brown first 2 ingredients together; drain. Stir in salsa and one cup Cheddar cheese; set aside. Combine sour cream, cayenne pepper, cumin and remaining Cheddar cheese together; set aside. Cover the bottom of an ungreased 13"x9" baking pan with 2 tortillas; spread with a layer of the sour cream mixture. Add a layer of meat mixture, then enchilada sauce. Repeat layers twice; sprinkle with chiles and remaining cheese. Cover with aluminum foil; bake at 350 degrees for 45 to 60 minutes. Uncover and bake 15 additional minutes; set aside for 20 minutes before serving. Makes 20 servings.

Make clean-up extra easy. Drape a paper tablecloth over the table, and use paper plates and plastic utensils. Decorate with wrapping paper strips, stickers and markers, then write guests' names right on the tablecloth for easy placecards. When dinner's done, just roll everything up and toss!

Desserts in a Dash

Creamy Peanut Butter Pie

Michelle Greeley
Hayes, VA

Whip up this no-bake dessert in minutes!

8-oz. pkg. cream cheese, softened
1/2 c. sugar
1/3 c. creamy peanut butter

1/3 c. frozen whipped topping, thawed
10 peanut butter cups, coarsely chopped and divided
9-inch chocolate pie crust

Blend cream cheese, sugar and peanut butter together until smooth; fold in whipped topping and half the chopped peanut butter cups. Spread into crust; sprinkle with remaining chopped peanut butter cups. Refrigerate until firm. Serves 6 to 8.

Give pies extra pizazz when company's coming.
Pour melted chocolate onto wax paper, spread into
a 3-inch wide strip and let stand until cool but not
firm. Pull a vegetable peeler across chocolate
and arrange curls on top of pies.

Desserts in a Dash

Banana Cream Pie

Rachelle Santamaria-Lao
Moreno Valley, CA

Sometimes we top with whipped cream and chocolate jimmies.

1/4 c. sugar
3 T. cornstarch
1-1/2 c. milk
2 egg yolks

1 T. butter
1/2 t. vanilla extract
2 bananas, sliced
9-inch pie crust, baked

Combine sugar and cornstarch in a double boiler; add milk. Heat and stir until mixture thickens; remove from heat. Slowly mix in egg yolks; return to heat, stirring until thickened. Stir in butter and vanilla; remove from heat. Set aside to cool. Layer banana slices over the bottom of the pie crust; pour sugar mixture on top. Bake at 400 degrees until golden, about 10 minutes; set aside to cool. Makes 8 servings.

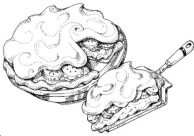

Banana Cupcakes

Debbie Donaldson
Florala, AL

Handed-down recipes are so special...this one is from my mother and it's one of the very first desserts I ever made.

1/3 c. butter
1 c. sugar
3 bananas, mashed
2 eggs, beaten

1/4 c. buttermilk
1 t. vanilla extract
1-1/2 c. self-rising flour
3/4 t. baking powder

Cream butter and sugar; mix in remaining ingredients. Fill paper-lined muffin cups 2/3 full with batter; bake at 325 degrees for 15 to 20 minutes. Makes 1-1/2 dozen.

Rainbow Cake

Wendy Lee Paffenroth
Pine Island, NY

Serve with a spoonful of whipped cream and sprinkling of strawberries for an extra-special treat.

16-oz. pkg. angel food cake mix
red, blue, yellow and green food
   coloring

Garnish: powdered sugar

Prepare cake mix following package directions; do not pour into tube pan. Place one cup batter into each of 4 different bowls; tint one pink, one blue, one yellow and one green. Spread pink batter into a greased and floured tube pan; carefully spoon blue batter on top. Repeat with yellow and then green batters; carefully place on lowest rack of oven, baking according to package directions. Remove from oven; invert onto a serving platter. Let cool; sprinkle with powdered sugar. Serves 10.

Decorating dessert plates is so easy and fun.
Try drizzling fruity syrups along the edges or pipe on
melted chocolate in fun designs and words. You can also
use simple kitchen utensils (forks work great) as
stencils...just lay them on the plate, sprinkle cocoa
or powdered sugar over top and remove to
show off designs. Clever!

Desserts in a Dash

Mom's Special Occasion Cherry Cake

Roger Baker
La Rue, OH

Mom always made this cake for birthdays, showers, anniversaries and the church ice cream social. Many times someone would offer to buy the whole cake before it could be cut and served!

2-1/4 c. cake flour
2-1/2 t. baking powder
1/4 t. salt
1/2 c. shortening
1-1/3 c. sugar
3 egg whites, beaten

2/3 c. milk
10-oz. jar maraschino cherries, drained with juice reserved
1/2 c. chopped walnuts
4-oz. jar maraschino cherries with stems

Combine flour, baking powder and salt in a small mixing bowl; set aside. Blend shortening in a large mixing bowl for 30 seconds; mix in sugar. Gradually add egg whites, blending well after each addition; set aside. Whisk milk and 1/4 cup reserved cherry juice together; add alternately with flour mixture to sugar mixture, mixing well. Fold in nuts and drained cherries; divide batter evenly and pour into 2 lightly greased and floured 8" round baking pans. Bake at 350 degrees for 25 to 30 minutes; cool on a wire rack for 10 minutes. Remove from pans to cool completely; frost bottom layer with butter frosting. Add top layer; frost. Decorate the top with a ring of stemmed cherries. Makes 8 to 10 servings.

Butter Frosting:

3/4 c. butter, softened
6 c. powdered sugar, divided
1/3 c. milk

1/4 t. salt
1-1/2 t. vanilla extract
4 to 6 drops red food coloring

Blend butter until fluffy; mix in 3 cups powdered sugar. Gradually blend in milk, salt and vanilla; add remaining powdered sugar, mixing well. Stir in food coloring to desired tint.

Crispy Graham Delights

Ginny Shaver
Avon, NY

These are great for putting together when friends drop in or the family needs something yummy fast!

graham crackers
1/2 c. sugar
1/2 c. butter

1/2 c. margarine
1/2 c. chopped pecans or
   walnuts

Line the bottom of an ungreased jelly-roll pan with one layer graham crackers; set aside. Place sugar, butter and margarine in a saucepan; bring to a boil and boil for one minute. Pour over graham crackers; spread to cover evenly. Sprinkle with pecans or walnuts; bake at 325 degrees until golden and bubbly, about 5 to 9 minutes. Cool slightly; remove with spatula and set aside to cool completely. Gently break into squares; store in an airtight container. Makes 2 dozen.

Bake 2 batches of Crispy Graham Delights and wrap several in brightly colored cellophane bags to send home with each guest...a double delight!

Desserts in a Dash

4-Layer Cookie Bars

Angela Hunker
Fostoria, OH

A crunchy and creamy dessert everyone will enjoy.

16-oz. pkg. rectangular buttery
   crackers
1/2 c. margarine
2/3 c. sugar
1/2 c. brown sugar, packed

1 c. graham cracker crumbs
1/4 c. milk
2/3 c. creamy peanut butter
1/2 c. chocolate chips
1/2 c. peanut butter chips

Line the bottom of a buttered 13"x9" baking pan with a single layer of crackers; set aside. Melt margarine in a heavy saucepan; add sugars, graham cracker crumbs and milk. Heat over medium-high heat until sugars dissolve, stirring often; spread over crackers. Arrange another single layer of crackers on top; set aside. Combine remaining ingredients in a saucepan; heat over low heat until melted, stirring until smooth and creamy. Spread over crackers; set aside until firm. Cut into bars to serve. Makes 2 dozen.

Short on table space? Use the kitchen counter for a buffet line, clear off a bookshelf for a self-serve beverage bar and use end tables for desserts.

Easy-Time Dessert Squares

Sharon Murray
Lexington Park, MD

Switch it every time...top with blueberry, strawberry or apricot pie filling.

1-1/2 c. sugar
1 c. margarine
4 eggs
2 c. all-purpose flour

1 t. lemon juice
21-oz. can cherry pie filling
Garnish: powdered sugar

Cream sugar and margarine until light and fluffy; add eggs, one at a time, mixing well after each addition. Blend in flour and lemon juice; spread in a greased jelly-roll pan. Score dough into squares with a table knife; spoon one heaping teaspoon cherry pie filling in the center of each square. Bake at 350 degrees until golden, about 25 to 30 minutes. Cool slightly; sprinkle with powdered sugar. Cool completely; cut into squares along scored lines. Makes 3 dozen.

Paper baking cups are available in many sizes
and are a great way to serve individual
desserts...especially for those ooey-gooey treats!

Desserts in a Dash

Sunny Lemon Bars

Kris Warner
Circleville, OH

Place cut bars in a freezer bag and freeze up to one month.
Thaw, covered, in the refrigerator before serving.

1-1/2 c. plus 3 T. all-purpose
    flour, divided
2/3 c. powdered sugar
3/4 c. butter, softened

3 eggs, beaten
1-1/2 c. sugar
1/4 c. lemon juice
Garnish: powdered sugar

Combine 1-1/2 cups flour, powdered sugar and butter; mix well.
Pat into a greased 13"x9" baking pan; bake at 350 degrees for
20 minutes. Whisk remaining flour, eggs, sugar and lemon juice
together until frothy; pour over hot crust. Bake until golden, about
20 additional minutes; cool on a wire rack. Dust with powdered sugar;
cut into bars to serve. Makes 2-1/2 dozen.

Strawberry-Banana Sherbet

Linda Nowak
Cheektowaga, NY

So easy to make and serve...just pop a few frozen cubes in a bowl
and add a spoon!

4 c. strawberries, hulled and
    sliced
4 ripe bananas
1/2 c. sugar

1 c. orange juice
3 T. lemon juice
2 c. milk

Mash strawberries in a large bowl; set aside. Mash bananas and sugar
in a medium bowl until smooth; add to strawberries, mixing well. Stir
in orange juice, lemon juice and milk. Divide mixture between 4 ice
cube trays; freeze about 4 hours. Serves 6 to 8.

Brownies à la Mode

Judy Borecky
Escondido, CA

I've been using this recipe since the 1960's and I have revised it over the years into this yummy dessert. It's so simple, but fit for extra-special company.

1-1/2 c. all-purpose flour
1/2 t. baking powder
1/2 t. salt
1/3 c. baking cocoa
2 c. sugar
1 c. butter, softened

4 eggs, beaten
1/2 c. chocolate chips
1/4 c. chopped nuts
vanilla ice cream
Garnish: caramel ice cream
    topping and chocolate syrup

Combine the first 5 ingredients together; toss gently to mix. Stir in butter and eggs; blend well. Spread batter into a greased 13"x9" baking pan; sprinkle with chocolate chips and nuts. Bake at 350 degrees for 30 to 35 minutes; cool to lukewarm. Cut into squares and top each with a scoop of ice cream; drizzle with caramel topping and chocolate syrup. Makes 2 dozen.

Host a pile-it-on ice cream social! Alongside Brownies à la Mode, set out Mason jars filled with yummy toppings like chocolate candies, butterscotch chips, raspberries, cherries, hot fudge and creamy caramel...guests can even bring their favorite to share.

Desserts in a Dash

Chocolate-Peanut Butter Brownies *Jennifer Dutcher*
Lewis Center, OH

Chocolate and peanut butter...two reasons these brownies will disappear fast!

4 1-oz. sqs. bittersweet baking
   chocolate
3/4 c. butter
2 c. sugar
3 eggs, beaten

2 t. vanilla extract, divided
1 c. all-purpose flour
1 c. peanuts, chopped
1 c. creamy peanut butter
1/2 c. powdered sugar

Place chocolate and butter in a microwave-safe bowl; microwave until butter melts, stirring often. Add to a medium mixing bowl; blend in sugar, eggs and one teaspoon vanilla. Mix in flour and peanuts; spread in a greased 13"x9" baking pan. Bake at 350 degrees for 25 to 30 minutes; cool. Blend peanut butter, powdered sugar and remaining vanilla until smooth and creamy; spread over brownies. Drizzle with glaze; set aside until firm. Cut into squares to serve. Makes 2 dozen.

Glaze:

4 1-oz. sqs. semi-sweet baking
   chocolate

1/4 c. butter

Melt ingredients together; stir until creamy.

For a change of pace, try serving dessert around the coffee table...everyone can sit on big fluffy cushions.

Time-Saver Chocolate Cake

Carol Golden
Plantersville, TX

Quick and scrumptious!

2 c. all-purpose flour	1 t. vanilla extract
2 c. sugar	1/2 c. buttermilk
1/4 c. baking cocoa	1/2 t. baking soda
1/2 c. margarine	1 t. cinnamon
1 c. water	2 eggs

Combine flour and sugar in a large mixing bowl; set aside. Add baking cocoa, margarine, water and vanilla to a saucepan; bring to a boil, stirring often. Remove from heat; pour into flour mixture. Add remaining ingredients; mix well. Spread in a greased and floured 13"x9" baking pan; bake at 350 degrees until a toothpick inserted in the center removes clean, about 30 minutes. Remove from oven; spread frosting over warm cake. Cut into squares to serve. Makes 24 servings.

Frosting:

1/2 c. margarine	1/4 c. baking cocoa
6 T. milk	1-lb. pkg. powdered sugar

Place margarine, milk and baking cocoa in a saucepan; bring to a boil, stirring constantly. Remove from heat; stir in powdered sugar until smooth and creamy.

For instant cheer, string 4 to 5 helium balloons and tie them to a small bag filled with marbles or sand. Place the bag in the center of a Bundt® cake and let the balloons float overhead.

Desserts in a Dash

Double Berry Cake

Laurie Park
Westerville, OH

After baking, fill this cake's center with a variety of fresh berries, whipped topping or vanilla pudding to spoon over each slice for an extra-special treat.

2 c. all-purpose flour
1 T. baking powder
1 t. baking soda
1/4 t. salt
1 c. sugar
1/4 t. nutmeg

3/4 c. buttermilk
1/2 c. egg substitute
1/4 c. oil
2 c. frozen raspberries, thawed
2 c. frozen blueberries, thawed

Combine flour, baking powder, baking soda and salt in a large mixing bowl; set aside. Stir sugar, nutmeg, buttermilk, egg substitute and oil together; add to flour mixture, stirring until just moistened. Fold in raspberries and blueberries; spread in a greased 6-cup Bundt® pan. Bake at 350 degrees until a toothpick inserted in the center removes clean, about one hour; cool on a wire rack. Remove cake to a serving platter. Serves 12.

A piece-of-cake centerpiece! A cake stand does double duty as a simple platform for chunky candles...wrap a ribbon around each pillar for added color and charm.

Tropical Cakes

*Cindy Colley
Othello, WA*

*This recipe makes 2 cakes...one to share right away and one to freeze
for unexpected company. Just save the coconut
to sprinkle on right before serving.*

18-1/2 oz. pkg. yellow cake mix
3 3.4-oz. pkgs. instant vanilla
   pudding mix
3-1/2 c. milk
1-1/2 t. coconut extract
20-oz. can crushed pineapple,
   drained with juice reserved

8-oz. pkg. cream cheese,
   softened
16-oz. container frozen whipped
   topping, thawed
2 c. flaked coconut, toasted

Prepare cake mix according to package directions; divide batter evenly
between 2 greased 13"x9" baking pans. Bake at 350 degrees for
15 minutes; cool completely. Combine pudding mixes, milk, coconut
extract and reserved pineapple juice in a large mixing bowl; blend for
2 minutes. Mix in cream cheese; fold in pineapple. Spread over cakes;
top with a layer of whipped topping. May freeze up to one month or
sprinkle with coconut and refrigerate for at least 2 hours. Makes
36 servings.

Create a super cool
centerpiece for a dessert
party. Clean an empty ice
cream container (or ask the
local store for extras), fill
with floral foam and tuck
in some bright flowers.

Desserts in a Dash

Peaches & Cream Pie

Sydney Taylor
Roanoke, VA

Bursting with flavor, this dessert is special enough for any occasion.

3/4 c. self-rising flour
2-3/4 oz. pkg. cook & serve
   vanilla pudding mix
3 T. margarine
1 egg
1/2 c. milk

28-oz. can sliced peaches,
   drained with juice reserved
8-oz. pkg. cream cheese,
   softened
1 c. plus 1 T. sugar, divided
1/2 t. cinnamon

Combine the first 5 ingredients; mix well. Pour into a buttered 10" glass pie pan; arrange peaches on top. Set aside. Blend cream cheese, 3 tablespoons reserved peach juice and one cup sugar until smooth and creamy; spread over peaches to within one inch of the edge. Sprinkle with remaining sugar and cinnamon; bake at 350 degrees for 30 to 35 minutes. Serves 8.

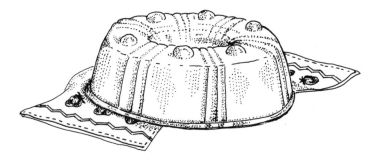

When thinking of centerpieces, remember to use larger, more showy arrangements on a buffet table and smaller ones on the dining table so guests can easily talk.

Sprinkle-Swirl Brownies

Rebecca Miller
Union Star, MO

Try sprinkling with chocolate chips, crushed butterscotch candy or peanut butter chips during the last 5 minutes of baking...delightful!

2 c. sugar
3/4 c. baking cocoa
1/2 t. baking powder
1-1/2 c. all-purpose flour

1/2 t. salt
2 t. vanilla extract
5 eggs
1 c. butter, softened

Combine the first 5 ingredients in a large mixing bowl; gradually blend in remaining ingredients. Spread batter in a greased 13"x9" baking pan; drop cream mixture by tablespoonfuls onto the batter. Swirl with a knife through the batter; bake at 350 degrees for 20 to 30 minutes. Makes 2 dozen.

Cream Mixture:
Blend all ingredients together until smooth and creamy.

1/2 c. cream cheese, softened
1/2 c. powdered sugar

1 T. all-purpose flour
1 to 2 T. milk

Tiny bud vases grouped together or used singly make a sweet addition to any dessert table.

Desserts in a Dash

No-Bother, No-Bake Cheesecake

Carla Turner
Salem, OR

Try putting half the filling in the crust, spread a thin layer of jam on top, then add remaining filling.

8-oz. pkg. cream cheese,
   softened
1/3 c. sugar
1 c. sour cream

2 t. vanilla extract
8-oz. container frozen whipped
   topping, thawed
9-inch graham cracker pie crust

Blend cream cheese and sugar until light and fluffy; mix in sour cream. Add vanilla and whipped topping; mix well. Spread into pie crust; refrigerate until set, about 3 to 4 hours. Makes 8 servings.

Yummy No-Crust Cheesecake

Mary Lauff-Thompson
Philadelphia, PA

A pudding-like treat.

2 8-oz. pkgs. cream cheese,
   softened
1 c. sugar
4 eggs

1 c. milk
2 t. cornstarch
1 t. vanilla extract
1/2 t. cinnamon

Blend cream cheese, sugar and eggs together; mix in milk, cornstarch and vanilla. Spread in a buttered and lightly floured 8"x8" baking pan; sprinkle with cinnamon. Bake at 325 degrees for one hour; turn off oven and leave in for 5 additional minutes. Makes 16 servings.

Blueberry-Sour Cream Cake

Kathy Grashoff
Fort Wayne, IN

Homebaked goodness in a hurry!

1-1/2 c. all-purpose flour
1 c. sugar, divided
1/2 c. butter, softened
1-1/2 t. baking powder
1 egg

2 t. vanilla extract, divided
1 qt. blueberries
2 c. sour cream
2 egg yolks

Combine flour, 1/2 cup sugar, butter, baking powder, egg and one teaspoon vanilla; mix thoroughly. Spread batter in a greased 9"x9" baking pan; sprinkle with blueberries. Set aside. Blend sour cream, egg yolks, remaining sugar and vanilla together; pour over blueberries. Bake at 350 degrees for one hour. Serves 9.

Cute on cakes, cookies or cupcakes...stack up 2 or 3 round fruit-flavored candies to use as holders for celebration candles.

Desserts in a Dash

Streusel-Topped Raspberry Bars

Rogene Rogers
Bemidji, MN

Guaranteed smiles!

2-1/4 c. all-purpose flour
1 c. sugar
1 c. chopped pecans

1 c. butter, softened
1 egg
3/4 c. raspberry preserves

Combine first 5 ingredients together in a large mixing bowl; blend
on low speed until mixture resembles coarse crumbs, about 2 to
3 minutes. Reserve 2 cups mixture; set aside. Place remaining crumb
mixture in a greased 9"x9" baking pan; press to cover the bottom.
Spread raspberry preserves to within 1/2 inch from the edges; crumble
reserved crumb mixture over the top. Bake at 350 degrees for 40 to
50 minutes; cool completely. Cut into bars to serve. Makes about
2 dozen.

Old-fashioned gelatin molds, tart tins and vintage
drinking glasses are just right for filling with
bite-size candies...place several around the
room for easy snacking.

Slice & Bake Cookies

Kathleen Shockey
Wichita, KS

*Make now and freeze...just thaw, slice and bake
as friends drop by.*

2 c. butter, softened
2 c. sugar
2 eggs
5 c. all-purpose flour, divided
1 t. baking soda

8-oz. pkg. candied red
   cherries, diced
8-oz. pkg. candied green
   cherries, diced
2 c. chopped pecans

Cream butter and sugar until fluffy; blend in eggs, 4 cups flour
and baking soda. Set aside. Gently toss cherries with remaining flour;
fold into dough. Stir in pecans; mix thoroughly. Divide dough into
5 portions; form each into a roll. Double wrap in plastic wrap, if
desired; either freeze until ready to bake or slice into 1/4-inch thick
slices and arrange on ungreased baking sheets. Bake at 350 degrees
for 5 to 10 minutes. Makes about 8 to 9 dozen.

Quick-Batch Peanut Butter Cookies *Janie Branstetter*
Duncan, OK

A favorite, quick & easy cookie...and surprise, no flour!

2 c. creamy peanut butter
2 c. sugar

2 eggs
2 t. vanilla extract

Combine all ingredients together; drop by teaspoonfuls on
ungreased baking sheets. Bake at 350 degrees for 10 minutes.
Makes 3 to 4 dozen.

Desserts in a Dash

Nana's Soft Jam Cookies

Michelle Moulder
The Woodlands, TX

Nana made these for my sisters and me all the time when we were little girls. We would walk down to her house on Saturdays and these mouth-watering delights would be in the oven. Now I often make them for my family...we always have a variety of flavors since you can use all your favorite jams.

1-1/2 c. all-purpose flour	1 egg
1/2 t. salt	1 t. vanilla extract
1/4 t. baking soda	1/2 c. sugar
1/2 c. oil	assorted flavored jams

Combine flour, salt and baking soda in a medium mixing bowl; set aside. Blend oil, egg, vanilla and sugar together in a large mixing bowl; mix in flour mixture. Drop by teaspoonfuls 1/2 inch apart on an ungreased baking sheet; make an indentation with the back of a small spoon in the center of each cookie. Place 1/2 teaspoon jam in the depressions; bake at 375 degrees for 8 to 10 minutes. Cool one to 2 minutes; remove to wire racks to cool completely. Makes 2 dozen.

I am still convinced that a good, simple, homemade cookie is preferable to all the store-bought cookies one can find.
- James Beard

Slow-Cooker Cherry Tapioca

Susan Estel
New Egypt, NJ

Such a fresh taste...friends will love it!

2 qts. milk
10-oz. jar maraschino cherries,
   drained and chopped with
   juice reserved
1 c. pearl tapioca

1-1/4 c. sugar
4 eggs, beaten
1 t. vanilla extract
Garnish: frozen whipped
   topping, thawed

Combine milk, 1/2 cup reserved cherry juice, sugar and tapioca; pour into a slow cooker. Heat on high setting for 3 hours. Blend eggs and vanilla together; add 1/4 cup liquid from slow cooker. Mix well; pour egg mixture into slow cooker. Heat on high setting, uncovered, until thickened, about 15 to 20 minutes. Stir in cherries; refrigerate until chilled. Serve with a dollop of whipped topping. Serves 8.

Who says glasses should be reserved for beverages?
Elegant stemmed glasses are just right for serving up
desserts like ice cream, tapioca, pudding and mousse...and
it's sure to make guests feel extra special.

Desserts in a Dash

Lemon Pudding

Dorothy Baldauf
Crystal Lake, IL

This light dessert recipe has been in the family for years.
The sweet-tart taste makes a great ending to any meal.

1 c. sugar
2 T. butter
2 T. all-purpose flour

zest and juice of 1-1/2 lemons
2 eggs, divided
1 c. milk

Cream sugar and butter; mix in flour. Add lemon zest and juice; blend well. Mix in egg yolks and milk; set aside. Whip egg whites until stiff peaks form; fold into lemon mixture. Pour into a buttered one-quart casserole dish; set in a shallow baking pan filled with 1/2 inch water. Bake at 350 degrees for 35 minutes. Serves 6.

Lemon Vanilla Bark

Deborah Ludke
Glenville, NY

Joining friends for dinner at their place? Take a tin full of this bark to
give to your hostess.

4 1-oz. sqs. white melting
  chocolate, chopped

4-oz. pkg. hard lemon candies,
  coarsely crushed

Place chocolate in a microwave-safe bowl; melt according to package directions. Stir in 3/4 of the crushed lemon candies; spread in a jelly-roll pan sprayed with non-stick vegetable spray. Sprinkle remaining crushed candy on top, pressing lightly; refrigerate until firm. Break apart and store in an airtight container. Makes about 1/2 pound.

Red Velvet Cake

Jennifer Bryant
Bowling Green, KY

Scrumptiously rich...top with white chocolate curls for a special touch.

1/2 c. butter, softened
1-1/2 c. sugar
2 eggs
2-oz. bottle red food coloring
2 T. baking cocoa
1 c. buttermilk

2-1/4 c. self-rising flour
1/2 t. salt
1 t. vanilla extract
1 t. baking soda
1 T. vinegar

Cream butter and sugar together; add eggs, blending well. Set aside. Stir food coloring and cocoa together to make a paste; mix into creamed mixture. Add buttermilk, flour and salt; blend well. Set aside. Stir vanilla, baking soda and vinegar together; fold into batter. Pour batter equally into 3 greased and floured 8" round baking pans; bake at 325 degrees for 25 to 30 minutes. Cool; place first layer on serving platter and frost. Add second layer and frost; repeat with third layer, frosting top and sides. Makes 10 to 12 servings.

Icing:

8-oz. pkg. cream cheese,
   softened
1/2 c. margarine, softened

1 t. vanilla extract
1-lb. pkg. powdered sugar

Blend all ingredients together until smooth and creamy.

Wrap a wide ribbon around a tall, layered cake and tie a bow in the front. So simple and elegant!

Desserts in a Dash

Classic Carrot Cake

Janet Allen
Hauser, ID

Sprinkle cinnamon and chopped walnuts over top...so pretty!

4 eggs
1-3/4 c. sugar
1 c. oil
2 c. all-purpose flour
2 t. baking soda
1 t. salt

1 t. cinnamon
1-1/2 carrots, shredded
1 c. apple, cored, peeled and
   coarsely chopped
1/2 c. chopped walnuts

Blend eggs, sugar and oil together; set aside. Combine flour, baking soda, salt and cinnamon; mix into egg mixture. Stir in carrots, apple and walnuts; pour into 2 greased and floured 9" round baking pans. Bake at 350 degrees for 30 to 35 minutes or until a toothpick inserted in the center removes clean; cool on wire racks for 10 minutes. Remove from pans; cool completely. Arrange one layer on a serving plate; frost with cream cheese frosting. Add second layer; frost top and sides. Makes 10 to 12 servings.

Cream Cheese Frosting:

8-oz. pkg. cream cheese,
   softened
1/2 c. butter, softened

2 t. vanilla extract
4-1/2 to 5 c. powdered sugar

Blend cream cheese, butter and vanilla together until fluffy; gradually mix in powdered sugar until smooth.

Microwave Chocolate Pudding

Justina Montoya
Belen, NM

The perfect ending to casual meals year 'round.

2/3 c. sugar
1/4 c. baking cocoa
3 T. cornstarch
1/4 t. salt

2-1/4 c. milk
2 T. butter, softened
1 t. vanilla extract

Combine first 4 ingredients in a microwave-safe mixing bowl; gradually stir in milk. Microwave on high for 6 minutes, stirring every 2 minutes. Stir in butter and vanilla until smooth. Divide pudding into 4 individual serving dishes; press plastic wrap directly onto pudding surface in each dish. Chill 3 to 4 hours. Serves 4.

No-Bake Peanut Butter Oaties

Christie Sanders
Grapeland, TX

Oh-so good!

1-1/2 c. sugar
6 T. baking cocoa
1/2 c. margarine, melted
1/2 c. milk

1/2 to 3/4 c. creamy
    peanut butter
3 c. quick-cooking oats,
    uncooked

Combine sugar and cocoa in a saucepan; stir in margarine, milk and peanut butter. Bring to a boil over medium heat; boil for 1-1/2 minutes, stirring constantly. Remove from heat; add oats, stirring thoroughly. Drop by rounded teaspoonfuls onto wax paper; allow to set. Makes 3 dozen.

Desserts in a Dash

Chocolate Chip Cookie Pie

Ann Hess
Bloomsburg, PA

Serve warm with a scoop of ice cream!

2 eggs
1/2 c. sugar
1/2 c. brown sugar, packed
3/4 c. butter, softened

1/2 c. all-purpose flour
1 c. chocolate chips
Optional: 1 c. chopped walnuts
9-inch pie crust

Cream together eggs, sugar, brown sugar and butter; add flour, mixing well. Stir in chocolate chips and walnuts, if desired. Spread in pie crust; bake at 325 degrees for one hour, or until center tests done. Serves 6 to 8.

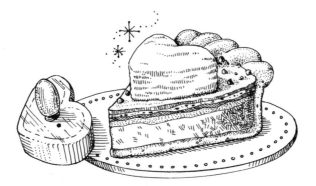

Really impress guests by serving ice cream cut-outs with dessert. Spoon softened ice cream 1/2-inch thick in a jelly-roll pan; freeze until firm. Use cookie cutters to cut out shapes and serve it on top of a slice of pie!

Oatmeal-Date Cookies

Doreen Dietz
Crystal Lake, IL

A special addition to any cookie platter.

1 c. butter, softened
1 c. brown sugar, packed
2 c. long-cooking oats,
    uncooked

2 c. all-purpose flour
1 t. baking powder
1/4 c. warm water

Mix all ingredients together; shape into forty-eight, 3/4-inch balls.
Arrange on an ungreased baking sheet; bake at 350 degrees for
10 minutes. Cool. Spread filling on flat sides of half the cookies; press
flat sides of remaining cookies on top of spread. Makes 2 dozen.

Filling:

8-oz. pkg. chopped dates
1 c. sugar

3 to 4 T. water

Place all ingredients in a small saucepan; heat until sugar dissolves,
stirring constantly. Remove from heat; set aside to cool slightly.

Set up a coffee station for friends to enjoy while nibbling
on dessert. Make it extra special by offering flavored
creamers, candied stirrers and scrumptious toppings like
whipped cream, cinnamon and chocolate shavings.

Desserts in a Dash

Orange-Spice Shortbread Cookies
Karrie Middaugh
Salt Lake City, UT

These cookies melt in your mouth...and they make your kitchen smell wonderful too!

2-1/4 c. all-purpose flour
2/3 c. sugar
1 t. orange zest
1/4 t. nutmeg

1/8 t. salt
1-1/4 c. chilled butter, sliced
Garnish: powdered sugar

Combine flour, sugar, zest, nutmeg and salt; cut in butter with a pastry cutter until coarse crumbs form. Form dough into a ball; divide in half. Press one portion into the bottom of a lightly greased 8"x8" baking pan; prick lightly with a fork at one-inch intervals. Repeat with remaining dough. Bake at 325 degrees for 30 to 35 minutes; immediately remove from pans. Cut into 2-inch squares with a pizza cutter; slice each square diagonally to form 2 triangles. Sprinkle with powdered sugar; cool completely. Makes about 5 dozen.

Cover up a less-than-charming serving plate with a paper doily before arranging cookies on top. Chic and cheap, paper doilies are easy to come by at the grocery or craft store.

Abracadabra Bars

Lisa Johnson
Hallsville, TX

7 layers of heaven!

1/2 c. butter, melted
1 c. graham cracker crumbs
1 c. milk chocolate chips
1 c. butterscotch chips

1 c. flaked coconut
1 c. chopped walnuts
14-oz. can sweetened
   condensed milk

Coat the bottom of 13"x9" baking pan with butter; sprinkle the next 5 ingredients on top in the order listed. Gently pour condensed milk over top; bake at 325 degrees for 25 minutes. Cool; cut into bars. Refrigerate until firm. Makes 2-1/2 dozen.

Don't forget to serve milk with dessert! Wrap printed napkins or bands of oilcloth around tall drinking glasses and secure with a sticker...you can even write guests' names on the stickers so they always know which glass is theirs.

Desserts in a Dash

Cream Cheese Crescent Bars

Lisa Delisi
Bristol, WI

I take this dessert to almost every event I attend...and I always bring copies of the recipe because I get so many requests.

2 8-oz. tubes crescent rolls, separated
2 8-oz. pkgs. cream cheese, softened

1 t. vanilla extract
2/3 c. sugar
1 egg, separated

Line the bottom of a greased 13"x9" baking pan with one package crescent rolls, pinching seams together; set aside. Blend cream cheese, vanilla, sugar and egg yolk together; spread evenly over crust. Gently place remaining crescent roll dough on top, pinching seams together; set aside. Whisk egg white until frothy; brush over the top of the dough. Sprinkle with topping; bake at 350 degrees until golden, about 25 to 30 minutes. Slice into bars to serve. Makes 2 dozen.

Topping:

1/2 c. sugar
1/4 c. chopped pecans

1 t. cinnamon

Gently toss all ingredients together.

A heaping plate of cookies, bars or cupcakes makes a delightful (and delicious) centerpiece at a casual gathering with friends...don't forget the napkins!

Soft Molasses Cookies

Jenn Vallimont
Port Matilda, PA

The key to softness is to not overbake.

1 c. shortening
1/4 c. molasses
1 c. brown sugar, packed
1 egg
2 t. baking soda
1/2 t. ground cloves

1/2 t. ground ginger
1 t. cinnamon
1/2 t. salt
2 c. all-purpose flour
1 c. sugar

Cream shortening, molasses, brown sugar and egg together in a large mixing bowl; set aside. Combine dry ingredients except for sugar in a medium mixing bowl; mix well. Gradually blend dry ingredients into creamed mixture; shape dough into a ball. Wrap in wax paper; refrigerate for at least 3 hours or overnight. Shape into walnut-size balls; roll in sugar. Place on ungreased baking sheets; bake at 375 degrees for 8 to 10 minutes. Makes about 5 dozen.

Show off your basket collection. Load up several with cookies and bars and arrange on the table.
Fill others with fresh flowers, and one with flatware rolled up in napkins. So cheery!

Desserts in a Dash

Peanut Butter Sweetie Cookies

Suzanne Stewart
Trumbull, CT

A tasty cookie I bake with my daughter, Molly...they're always a huge success!

1-3/4 c. all-purpose flour
1 t. baking soda
1/2 t. salt
1 c. sugar, divided
2 T. milk
1/2 c. brown sugar, packed

1/2 c. shortening
1/2 c. creamy peanut butter
1 egg
1 t. vanilla extract
6-oz. pkg. chocolate drops,
 unwrapped

Combine flour, baking soda, salt, 1/2 cup sugar, milk, brown sugar, shortening, peanut butter, egg and vanilla together; mix well. Shape into one-inch balls; roll in remaining sugar. Arrange on ungreased baking sheets; slightly flatten with the bottom of a glass dipped in sugar. Bake at 375 degrees for 10 minutes; place one chocolate drop in the center of each cookie. Cool. Makes about 3 dozen.

Surprise guests with a simple dessert. Whip up a few batches of homemade cookies and serve them in big glass cookie jars...just set them in the middle of the table and invite everyone to dig in!

Brownie Cupcakes

Robin Moyer
Fremont, NE

Make in mini muffin cups for one-bite brownies.

4 1-oz. sqs. semi-sweet baking
   chocolate
1 c. butter
1-1/2 c. chopped walnuts

1-3/4 c. sugar
1 c. all-purpose flour
4 eggs
1 t. vanilla extract

Melt chocolate and butter; stir in nuts and set aside. Combine sugar,
flour, eggs and vanilla; mix until well blended. Add to chocolate
mixture; mix until just blended. Spoon into paper-lined muffin cups;
bake at 325 degrees for 30 minutes. Makes one dozen.

Make dessert extra fun for the kids. Bake a
chocolate-covered mint patty inside one Brownie
Cupcake...whoever gets that one wins a prize!

Desserts in a Dash

Fudgy Chocolate-Raspberry Cake

Brad Daugherty
Gooseberry Patch

This has become the traditional "celebration cake" among my friends & family. Chocolate and raspberry are an unbeatable match, but this recipe works well with strawberry jam too!

18-1/4 oz. pkg. devil's food cake mix
1 c. water
1/3 c. oil
3 eggs
1 t. vanilla extract
1/4 c. sour cream
1 c. semi-sweet chocolate chips

Combine cake mix, water, oil, eggs, vanilla and sour cream in a large bowl; beat batter with an electric mixture for 2 minutes. Stir in chocolate chips. Divide batter evenly between 3 buttered 8" round cake pans. Bake at 350 degrees for 25 minutes or until centers test done. Cool cakes in pans for 15 minutes; turn out and cool completely. Place one layer on serving platter and frost; add second layer and frost. Repeat with third layer, frosting top and sides of cake. Makes 10 to 12 servings.

Frosting:

1/2 c. seedless raspberry jam
3 T. butter
3 c. semi-sweet chocolate chips
3/4 c. sour cream
2 c. powdered sugar

Bring raspberry jam and butter to a simmer in a heavy saucepan over medium heat; remove from heat. Immediately stir in chocolate chips; stir until melted. Mix in sour cream and powdered sugar; beat with an electric mixer until smooth.

Before frosting layered cakes, wrap individual layers in plastic wrap and freeze overnight. Remove and frost right away...it's so easy to spread frosting and the cake stays moist longer!

Mom's Slow-Cooker Apple Pie

Sonya Collett
Sioux City, IA

Nothing ends a meal quite like apple pie.

8 tart apples, cored, peeled and
   sliced
2 t. cinnamon
1/4 t. nutmeg
1/4 t. allspice
3/4 c. milk
5 T. chilled butter, divided

3/4 c. sugar
2 eggs
1 t. vanilla extract
1-1/2 c. biscuit baking mix,
   divided
1/2 c. brown sugar, packed

Gently toss apple slices with cinnamon, nutmeg and allspice; place in
the bottom of a slow cooker. Combine milk, 2 tablespoons butter,
sugar, eggs, vanilla and 1/2 cup biscuit baking mix; layer on top of
apple mixture. Mix remaining biscuit baking mix with brown sugar;
cut in remaining butter with a pastry cutter until crumbly. Sprinkle on
top of apple mixture; bake on low setting for 7 to 8 hours. Makes 8 to
10 servings.

Personalize each dessert. Fill a pastry bag with melted
caramel (or chocolate!) and drizzle designs on wax
paper...try hearts, stars and friends' initials. Freeze
caramel until firm, then use to top each
serving of pie, cake or pudding.

Desserts in a Dash

Apple-Nut Cake

Kim Malusky
Twinsburg, OH

An old-fashioned favorite...enjoy with a warm cup of cider.

1-3/4 c. sugar
1 t. salt
1-1/2 t. cinnamon
3 eggs
1 c. oil

2 c. all-purpose flour
1 t. baking soda
1 c. chopped nuts
6 to 8 apples, cored, peeled and
    thinly sliced

Combine first 3 ingredients; blend in eggs and oil. Set aside. Mix flour and baking soda together; add to sugar mixture. Fold in nuts and apple slices; spread in a greased 13"x9" baking pan. Bake at 350 degrees for 50 minutes. Makes 15 to 18 servings.

Fill your home with an inviting aroma. Core an apple, place on a baking sheet and sprinkle brown sugar inside. Heat in a low oven one hour before guests arrive. Also try adding apple pie spice to a pot of boiling water...just let simmer over low heat.

Mocha Brownie Cookies

Linda McTaggart
Ankeny, IA

My Grandma La Velle always had these cookies in her freezer to bring out when anyone stopped by...we couldn't wait to have them, we'd just eat them frozen!

6 T. butter	3/4 c. sugar
1-1/2 1-oz. sqs. unsweetened baking chocolate, melted	1 egg
	1 t. baking powder
6 T. buttermilk	1 t. vanilla extract
1/3 t. baking soda	1 c. plus 2 T. all-purpose flour

Combine all ingredients in order listed; mix well. Drop by tablespoonfuls onto ungreased baking sheets; bake at 350 degrees for 10 minutes. Cool; frost. Makes about 1-1/2 dozen.

Coffee Frosting:

5 c. powdered sugar	6 T. butter, softened
1/4 c. baking cocoa	1/3 c. prepared coffee

Combine the first 3 ingredients; gradually blend in coffee until desired spreading consistency is reached.

Nestle several Mocha Brownie Cookies inside coffee filters...set a few "bowls" around the table for guests to enjoy after dinner. So clever!

Desserts in a Dash

All-Occasion Iced Cut-Outs

Christi Miller
New Paris, PA

*These yummy cookies can even be decorated
and then frozen...this shiny-hard icing stays bright!*

3-1/2 c. all-purpose flour
2-1/2 t. baking powder
1/2 t. salt
2/3 c. butter, softened

1-1/2 c. sugar
2 eggs
1-1/2 t. vanilla extract
1 T. milk

Sift flour, baking powder and salt together; set aside. Cream butter and sugar; blend in eggs until fluffy. Add vanilla; blend in flour mixture and milk. Mix well; cover and refrigerate dough overnight. Roll dough out on a lightly floured surface to 1/4-inch thickness; cut into desired shapes using cookie cutters. Transfer to parchment paper-lined baking sheets; bake at 400 degrees until golden, about 8 to 10 minutes. Cool on wire racks; frost, if desired.

Shiny Hard Icing:

2 c. powdered sugar
4 t. corn syrup

4 t. water
food coloring

Blend all ingredients together until smooth and creamy, add additional equal portions corn syrup and water until desired spreading consistency is reached.

Index

Index

Desserts

Mains

Index

We've cooked up a whole collection of Gooseberry Patch® books!

Have a taste for more? Call us toll-free at

1-800-854-6673

We'll send you our latest catalog filled with kitchenware, candles, handmade quilts, gourmet goodies, enamelware, bowls, bubble night lights and our very own line of cookbooks, calendars and organizers!

Phone us:
1·800·854·6673

Fax us:
1·740·363·7225

Visit our website:
www.gooseberrypatch.com

Send us your favorite recipe!

*and the memory that makes it special for you!** If we select your recipe for a brand new **Gooseberry Patch** cookbook, your name will appear right along with it...and you'll receive a FREE copy of the book! Mail to:

Vickie & Jo Ann
Gooseberry Patch, Dept. Book
600 London Road
Delaware, Ohio 43015

*Please include the number of servings and all other necessary information!

223

meals made special 🍴 yummy recipes 🧁 sharing with friends 📖 making memories 🖼 pretty place settings 🍵 laughter 🧁 company's coming 🥨 gatherings at home 🍋 welcome 🍋 come as you are 🍪 cozy get-togethers 🥧 oh-so simple 🍷